BARBECUED RIBS, SMOKED BUTTS,
and Other Great Feeds

Originally published as
Barbecued Ribs
and Other Great Feeds

BARBECUED RIBS, SMOKED BUTTS,
and Other Great Feeds

JEANNE VOLTZ

ALFRED A. KNOPF, NEW YORK, 1996

This Is a Borzoi Book
Published by Alfred A. Knopf, Inc.

Copyright © 1990 by Jeanne Voltz
Illustrations copyright © 1990 by Incandescent Ink, Inc.

Photo Credits
v, 149: Ray Fisher, Miami *Herald*
ii: Tony Garnet, Miami *Herald*
41: Steve March
256: Carmen Miranda in "The Gang's All Here": The Museum of
Modern Art

Illustration Credits
7, 10, 11, 13, 166: Maria Strosser

Library of Congress Cataloging-in-Publication Data
Voltz, Jeanne.
Barbecued ribs, smoked butts, and other great feeds.
(The Knopf cooks American series; 3)
Rev. ed. of: Barbecued ribs and other great feeds.   1985.
Includes bibliographical references (p. 262) and index.
1. Barbecue cookery.   I. Voltz, Jeanne. Barbecued ribs and
other great feeds.   II. Title.
TX840.B3V63   1990   641.5'784   89-43487
ISBN 0-394-58293-4
ISBN 0-679-76586-7(pbk.)

Manufactured in the United States of America

This work is a revised edition based on *Barbecued Ribs and Other
Great Feeds,* originally published by Alfred A. Knopf, Inc., in 1985.

Published June 29, 1990
First Paperback Edition, April 1996

For Luther Jr. and Jeanne Marie, who happily shared
our barbecue experiments

CONTENTS

PREFACE

As a bride and, a few years later, as a mother, I played a supporting role to an opinionated barbecue chef. In the fifties all husbands barbecued, with wives as chief assistants and errand girls.

Soon I began to give my advice—meat was too smoky, too black, overdone, or whatever—as I have my opinionated side, too. Early on my husband and I established that a woman can barbecue as well as a man. What a woman lacks in showmanship is made up for by a feel for detail such as discreet use of sauces and sensing when food is done.

Luther's and my last meal together was barbecued ribs in a garden in Florida, our second time living there. We had started out barbecuing together 20 years earlier when it was big stuff. We never missed a beat through the sixties and seventies, when only diehards breathed smoke to cook. When the barbecue bug bit again in the eighties, I was in practice, from doing it in the soft, balmy climes of South Florida, in breeze-kissed evenings in California, and on a ninth-floor terrace in an apartment building in New York City. Yes, I fired up a tabletop kettle and cooked ribs, lamb, chicken, and fish for guests on occasion.

A beau from my youth, Frank, looked me up in the mid-eighties, one thing led to another, and we were married and came to the North Carolina Piedmont. A large barbecue grill was a wedding present. Frank can go as crazy as anybody about barbecuing or smoking food—and he's a great fire builder. I must admit that one of the three cookers on the deck is gas-fueled. It starts easily, but provides enough uncertainties that cooking still is a grand adventure, cool breezes, rain, and humid weather being variously with us. But the deck is just off the dining room, so we can flip chicken breasts or veal chops onto the grill and enjoy it, summer or

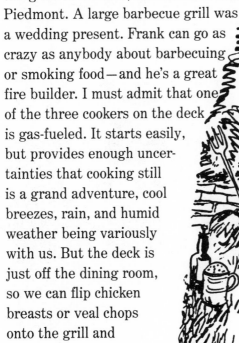

winter. The smoker requires pounds of charcoal to do a pork butt or turkey breast, but my, are home-smoked fish, smoked butt, and turkey breast fantastic! We've even learned to simulate a North Carolina pig pickin' and a Texas-style brisket on the smoker.

Barbecuing is convivial cooking. No outdoor sport invites more kibitzers, whether we are in Florida, California, New York City, or North Carolina; we're nosy onlookers in Alabama, Georgia, and Texas, and at contests and festivals all over the country.

This book takes the best from hundreds, maybe thousands, of backyard barbecue adventures, a lifetime of great eating and fun at grills of all sorts and in all conditions. We've learned lots and had a peck of fun. We hope you have fun and great food, too.

PLANTATION BARBECUING IN TIMES PAST

"Lambs, pigs, and kids, when barbecued, are split in half along the backbone. The animals butchered at sundown, and cooled of animal heat, after washing down well, are laid upon clean, split sticks of green wood over a trench two feet deep, and a little wider, and as long as need be, in which green wood has previously been burned to coals. There the meat stays twelve hours—from midnight to noon next day, usually. It is basted steadily with salt water, applied with a clean mop, and turned over once only. Live coals are added as needed from the log fire kept burning a little way off. All this sounds simple, dead easy. Try it—it really is an art. The plantation barbecuer was a person of consequence—moreover few plantations could show a master of the art.... The loan of him was an act of special friendship—profitable always to the personage lent. Then as now there were free barbecuers, mostly white—but somehow their handiwork lacked a little of perfection."—*Dishes and Beverages of the Old South* by Martha McCulloch-Williams, facsimile of the original edition published in 1913, University of Tennessee Press, 1988.

ACKNOWLEDGMENTS

Food and cooking are acceptable, even favorite, topics of conversation in my part of the country, and barbecue is the heart of a body of folklore to keep scholars studying for years to come. I am fortunate to have heard the living word of hundreds of experts, actual or self-appointed. Each of them contributed a germ of wisdom to the lore that makes this book.

Those who shared information collected as professionals include Marlys Beilunski of the National Live Stock and Meat Board, Chicago, Illinois; Elizabeth Wunderlich, Texas Beef Council, Austin; Taryn Butler, North Carolina Pork Producers, Raleigh; Emmie S. Whitley, North Carolina Poultry Federation, Raleigh; Laurie Dineen of the American Bison Association, Denver, Colorado; and Caroline Stuart, Greenwich, Connecticut.

Frank MacKnight, my husband, built the fires, did a good deal of the cooking, and got into the spirit of "better next time" when culinary trials turned out substandard food. I express thanks to tasters John and Jeff MacKnight, Ed and Dorothy Ajemian, Lenny and Chris Bolane, and Donn and Virginia Tee.

To my editor, Judith Jones, high praise for pushing ever so patiently to get the manuscript done to meet a pressing deadline, yet keeping the book up to her high standards.

GETTING STARTED

Unpacking a new grill, attaching the legs with bolts and nuts provided, if the device is unassembled, and grilling the first steak or frankfurter is a thrill. But it is not quite that easy! Superb food comes with experience. You learn as you cook. First, read the instructions that come with the grill. These may consist of a few sentences on the carton or a detailed manual. A manual is your bible in the use and care of a grill for its lifetime, so put the manual away carefully and trust it will be at your fingertips when an unexpected problem arises. A manual will tell you how to encourage a balky fire, how to winterize a grill, store and care for it to prevent premature rust-out, and how to clean it for longtime good looks and service.

You will come to know your grill as well as

your kitchen range, how many charcoal briquets to use for steaks or burgers and how many more for ribs, how to direct dampers, and other techniques. The first time you want to balance a turkey breast on the spit and get it turning over the fire, the manual will give you good advice.

But first of all, choose barbecue equipment to suit your needs, wants, and budget.

THE GRILL

Some of the best barbecued chicken I ever had was cooked on an old oven rack set precariously on two stacks of bricks with the fire burning on the ground between the bricks. Elaborate equipment is not necessary for barbecuing, but a well-designed grill makes the job easier and more efficient.

The price of a serviceable grill ranges from $15 to $25 for a small, simple brazier to $300 plus for a large grill with gadgets and attachments. There are four types of grills:

The simplest is a brazier or hibachi—basically a tray or pot to hold the fire with a grill over it. This is set in a frame. Some frames fold, making them portable for picnics and tailgate parties. Basic open braziers have no vents or dampers and the height of the grill cannot be adjusted. But they are fine for building a fire or grilling a steak or frankfurters. They make economical use of a dozen or fewer briquets for fast-cooked food. They can also be made to work like a more elaborate grill by tenting food with heavy-duty aluminum foil to hold in heat or positioning a baffle of foil or cardboard to shield food from drafts. Some grills with hoods have vents and dampers in the firebox. Some allow the chef to raise or lower the grill to spread heat to better suit the job or sear steaks close to the fire. On a blustery day, a hood that can be turned to shut off wind prevents undue cooling of the cooking area. Barbecue putterers often manage to cook ribs and other long-cooking foods by tending the fire judiciously and turning the baffle as needed to make the most of the heat in this style of grill.

A third sort of grill is covered, creating an oven with charcoal or gas fire inside. Gas grills have ceramic or lava rocks in fireboxes to burn drips and make food smell and look barbecued. A covered grill shuts out enough air to keep the temperature hot and discourage flare-ups. Round grills with domed covers are called barbecue kettles and look like giant kettles on stilts. Rectangular grills with covers and on wheels are called grill wagons and can be trundled around like pushcarts. The heat control provided by the cover, vents, and dampers makes covered grills worthwhile to serious chefs. A cover also holds in smoke to capture maximum benefits of smoldering wood and herbs.

A fourth type of outdoor cooker is a water smoker, a modern adaptation of the Chinese smoke oven. The firebox sits deep in a bottomless metal drum. A pan of water is set just above the firebox, then racks for food above it. When the water pan is removed and a grill rack set directly over the fire, the smoker serves as a grill. See the chapter on smoking for more detail on use as a smoker.

Gas grills suit barbecue fans who have no time to build fires. Lighting a gas grill takes a moment and the grill is heated in 15 minutes, rather than the 30 to 45 required for a charcoal grill. Gas lines feed fuel into the bottom of the firebox, which is lined with lava rocks or ceramic or pumice briquets that diffuse the heat. A rack is above the diffuser layer and in some grills rack height is adjustable. Heat intensity is gauged by BTUs, the higher the hotter when gas is turned on full force, but even heat is not guaranteed by high BTU ratings. A gas grill may be fueled by bottled propane or natural gas. Do not use propane in a grill made for natural gas or vice versa.

Purists claim food cooked in gas grills lacks authentic flavor. Others tuck a packet of dampened wood chips on the hot rocks or ceramic to smoke the food and feel the benefits compensate for any deficiency in flavor.

In-house grills are in many new homes and remodeled kitchens. A countertop grill by Jenn-Air started the rage. Now GE and other manufacturers offer them. The grill will cook almost anything in this book with little smoke in the kitchen, thanks to a self-venting system. The flavor is not quite like charcoal outdoors, but it's great. After my brother installed this type of grill in his kitchen in San Francisco he never cooked meat except on the grill. I enjoyed steaks, slabs of country ham, grilled petrale sole, and sand dabs in his kitchen.

In shopping for a grill of any type, check for durable finish and sturdy handles, legs, and joints. Porcelain on steel, cast aluminum, stainless steel, or cast iron are durable, but none should be allowed to weather. Any grill should be equipped with a vinyl or heavy plastic cover to toss over it outdoors, and it should be moved to a garage or other covered storage in the winter.

Check for a sturdy base or wheeled carriage. Make sure the grill is tip-proof. Wheels should lock and unlock easily so that the grill won't skitter across a terrace when it is full of fire.

A spit, often an optional extra, is worthwhile for large pieces of meat and birds. Good spits may be purchased separately, too.

A firebox or grill that can be set up or down to position food where you want it is of great advantage, but fewer and fewer grills have this feature. If your grill rack cannot be repositioned, a skilled chef can control heat by learning to keep the fire burning slowly for foods that need longer cooking, having the fire hotter for searing.

Other attachments to a basic grill are optional: shelves at the edge of the grill, hooks for hanging tools, racks for roasts or corn. Some of these accessories can be bought separately. I prefer a work table or cart to hold sauce, tongs, and other gear. The silliest attachment, I thought, was a grill with an umbrella ... until the night my husband held the golf umbrella over the fire to finish a batch of shish kebabs during a surprise rainstorm.

THE ACCESSORIES

Barbecue accessories clutter the toolshed and your life if friends insist on giving you every wild gadget that comes along. Choose what you like and give the others to a thrift shop. These are essentials at our grill:

Long-handled tongs, fork, and wide spatula (to turn meats and lift vegetables, seldom for pancakes).

Mitts made of durable flame-resistant material. Welders' gloves are ideal. With these gloves, you can pick up burning charcoal briquets and push them into the fire. But giftware and linen manufacturers have become smarter, and make mitts that are functional, washable, and good looking.

A plant spritzer or spray bottle to squirt a flare-up lightly. I used a toy water pistol, but found the spray-mister works as well and is quicker to find among the tools and foods.

One or more basting brushes—a long-handled, fine-bristled paint-brush reserved for basting or a string dish mop works well. Some new all-plastic brushes are dishwasher safe and handsome, too.

Cookware: a drip pan to set in the firebox, saucepans, and a skillet or two for cooking or heating sauces. Disposable pans can be used, but I take pans from the kitchen and spritz them with non-stick cooking spray so that sooty residue washes off with a quick swish of a sudsy sponge. Before non-stick spray, I wrapped pans inside and out with foil to avoid a dirty scouring job.

Aprons, hot-pot lifters, and a poker or fireplace shovel to push around coals. I use a towel constantly, so I want an apron pocket or tie long enough for tucking in the towel.

A fire starter—an electric one to place among briquets to ignite them quickly or a metal chimney in which you build a small fire to put in the coals. Look for it in stores that sell outdoor equipment. If you are of the kindling and crushed paper starter school, forget other starters. (See section on starting the fire, pages 10–12.)

An instant-registering thermometer is in my pocket at all times. I can tell in a few seconds if a thick cut of meat or turkey breast is done or needs a tad more cooking.

A covered bin for briquets along with a special place in the toolshed to keep it. Rain, humidity, and charcoal make a sooty mess and spoil the charcoal for cooking.

Other useful, but optional, equipment:

A basket broiler, a hinged wire device that opens flat to fill and is then

instant meat thermometer

closed and locked to hold food steady. It is especially useful for foods that stick to the grill or crumble, or small items like chicken legs, scallops, or steaks and chops that are a nuisance to turn.

A set of skewers. Flat blades twisted into elongated corkscrew shapes hold food without slipping. Wood skewers must be soaked before using to prevent charring.

Racks for vegetables or small foods help organize space on a grill and keep food separated for even cooking, but are not necessary if you arrange corn or potatoes around the meat.

Don't skimp on aluminum foil, paper towels, and napkins on which to put a messy brush before you wash it, line a tray, or spread over salad while you wait for the meat to get done.

spritzer

skewers

fire starter

drip pan

GETTING STARTED

THE FUEL

Charcoal briquets, wood charcoal, or wood are standard for outdoor cooking. Mesquite, hickory, and fruit- and nutwoods are fine, but generally are too scarce to squander as cooking fuel. They are used as chips or chunks added in small amounts to a fire toward the end. But if you lose a tree to a winter storm or disease, an oak, hickory, or other good-burning wood, dry it and have it cut as fuel.

Briquets have it over wood and wood charcoal in that high-quality ones such as Bridgeford burn longer and hotter than wood or untreated charcoal. But there are poor briquets, too. A diligent barbecuer will try the briquets of the region, some of them excellent, to compare them with national brands before settling on one briquet.

Briquets are sawdust, fine wood chips, or other pulpy material that have been dried in an oven and compressed into bricklike squares; hence the name briquets. Their quality varies widely. Some burn hotter, some burn longer, some start more easily, and many are treated for easier lighting. Others have a crankcaselike smell due to excessive petroleum mastic to hold the pulp together, so a run-through of the briquets offered is a good idea.

Smell charcoal before you buy it. Sniff a torn bag. Briquets that smell strongly of petroleum may not cook away the odor before you put food on the fire. Heavily oiled briquets have a greasy feel and leave black smudges on your hands, though there is natural smudging from charcoal that will burn. Good-quality compressed wood briquets leave a powdery film on your hands, almost as light as the charcoal used in artwork. First-quality briquets have a clean, slightly burnt-wood aroma, with a faint scent of resin, as if a bit of fat pine lurks in it.

If you find an old-fashioned hardware store manager, you can bet he barbecues on the weekends, and he's usually glad to share his experience. The same is true of a supermarket man, and sometimes women in the stockroom will venture an opinion on briquets.

Every time we move we poll the neighbors and any local tradespeople who profess to know anything of barbecuing about briquets. And we've found some fine briquets this way. We test with a two-pound bag of each candidate. When we find a "best" one, we buy a 10- or 25-pound bag.

The tradition of special woods for special foods goes back centuries. When the white man first came to the Pacific Northwest, Native Americans were grilling salmon over alderwood fires, and outdoor cooks in Washington State still use alder for fish. Winegrowers in the California valleys have adopted the French custom of grilling delicate foods over dried vine cuttings. A Swedish hostess once warmed smoked salmon over fir boughs dipped into the Baltic Sea at her doorstep. I've tried this with juniper boughs and fresh pine cuttings for a faint scent of resin in the fish.

Mesquite grows like a weed in California and Southwestern desert lands. It is expensive to harvest from its wild environs, but burns hot and fragrantly for meats, poultry, and game. We think it gives fish a bitter tang, so we save it for other foods.

Hickory provides an intense smoky aroma, the preferred flavor for barbecued ribs, pork roasts, poultry, beef, and lamb. Pecan or walnut, in case you fall heir to these woods, give off smoky aromas that do wonders for most meats. But don't let a hickory fire flame up. It leaves a smoky residue that is most unappetizing on food.

Apple- and cherrywood chips or chunks provide a fruity smoke and are good on chicken, turkey, pork, and smoked hams or sausages. In New England applewood–smoked turkey is an autumn tradition. Applewood gives meat a faint golden color and cherrywood turns meat reddish brown. Plugs cut from wine barrels or distillery barrels (Jack Daniels, for one) are novel smoking woods.

Twigs or branches cut from shrubs in your garden can be used to flavor grilled meat. Be sure the wood is nonpoisonous (no oleander or poison ivy, please!) and nonresinous (no pine or fir for cooking, only for fast-heating salmon). Twigs sprayed recently with pesticides should not be used.

Kindling sticks are the important exception to nonresinous woods. They come in gift packs now and are used to start a wood or charcoal fire. Like liquid fire starters, use them early and let the resinous sap burn off before food goes on the fire.

In South Florida it is customary to toss a few prunings of Australian pine on a fire to scent the food. This is not a true pine, but a casuarina. When we lived there we clipped the feathery branch tips, soaked them in water, and put them on the fire 10 to 15 minutes before pork or chicken was done.

So learn your landscape trees and shrubs if you want to be creative about smoking scents. For safety, buy the bags of smoking chips and chunks that are available anywhere that fuel and barbecue equipment are sold.

THE FIRE

Building a good fire and keeping it at peak cooking condition defeat many stouthearted barbecue chefs, so don't despair if you have a few false starts. Start the fire at least 30 minutes before you plan to cook—better, 45 minutes. Let it burn down until coals glow red through a cover of gray ash. Now it is ready. To toss meat on a blazing fire produces meat that is blackened on the outside and covered with sooty fat but raw inside.

The other common error of barbecue fires is using too much charcoal. This is wasteful (and briquets are expensive fuel). Too many hot coals burn food to a black ghost of itself, too often dried beyond good eating quality. Think small for grilled food, and keep your fire moderate for long-cooked barbecue such as ribs or beef brisket.

Before starting a fire, brush away ashes in the fire pan, as ashes block air circulation and, if thick, fly when the fire is poked and settle on food.

Adjust dampers and vents for maximum ventilation to start the fire, and turn the grill or hood to catch the best breeze. On a windy day, it is best to turn the grill or hood to shield the fire. You'll get the feel of it as the fire starts to burn.

If a grill has no vents and dampers, set it to catch the best breeze for starting the fire; if air is very still and the fire balky, a fireplace bellows or folded newspaper fanned briskly will help feed it oxygen to get it burning. After the fire is started a grill with no vents can be shielded from too much draft with a piece of plywood or other screen. Anything will do—we once rigged up a child's blackboard to protect the fire from wind.

Lay the fire loosely in the firebox. Lining the firebox with foil helps cleanup later and reflects and intensifies heat slightly, but I like the glowing coals against the dark firebox and we hose out the firebox now and then. First crumple two or three sheets of newspaper and place them in the bottom of the firebox loosely to form pockets that let flames lick through the base freely. Crisscross kindling sticks or twigs over the paper or arrange them in a small tepee shape. We like "lighter knots," sticks of resinous pine, but small fast-burning dry twigs are quick lighters available at camp grounds and in landscapes with trees.

Arrange a few briquets over

and between kindling pieces, using 10 to 15 for a small to medium firebox; or to cook a couple of steaks or pieces of chicken, perhaps 20 for a larger firebox; or to cook two or three chickens, ribs, or a brisket. Add more briquets after the fire is burning well and before food is put on it.

An electric fire starter gets a fire going fast, and lights without paper and kindling. For a fast start, we use kindling plus electric starter, pushing the heater end of the starter into the laid fire. Follow the manufacturer's directions, but generally you should remove the starter as soon as the fire is catching.

When briquets are blazing furiously, adjust dampers and hood to direct ventilation as needed—and you're home free. For a long cooking job ahead, add more briquets now, so that they will be hot and covcovered with ash before you put food on the fire.

For a very long cooking job, and a great aid to keeping a smoker going, build an auxiliary fire in a smaller firepan. Transfer hot coals into the main fire as needed while cooking.

The fire starter is our choice for getting a fire going fast, but long matches touched into the base of the paper work fine. Some briquets labeled "fast-starting"

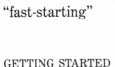

GETTING STARTED

are treated with fire starter. Liquid fire starters are best used sparingly and squirted on before you touch a light to the fire. Make sure petroleum fumes dissipate before you put food on the fire.

One way to use liquid starter is to soak three or four briquets in starter for a few minutes, then tuck them around the base of the fire. My imagination plays tricks, though, and if starter has been there I smell it in the food.

Never pour liquid fire starter on a smoldering fire. This is a fire prevention rule, and at this stage in the process the odor may not burn off before you are ready to cook.

Another method of starting a fire is with a lighter chimney, available in stores that sell grilling equipment. It is a metal cylinder about the size of a large juice can with holes in it. You start several briquets burning in it with newspaper as kindling, and then turn the minifire into the firebox of the grill as a core for your cooking fire.

We once made a home version of the chimney. With a beer-can opener we cut four wedges in the side at the bottom of a tomato juice can. We put four or five briquets in our "starter" and set it over a gas flame on the kitchen range. In a few minutes the minifire was ready to be put in the grill and topped with more briquets to build the fire. This is a compact fire, so open your grill vents and dampers full blast so the starter isn't smothered. And I warn you: You need very sturdy mitts for this operation to bring the gas-flamed fire from the kitchen to the grill safely.

Once the fire is started you can relax a minute or two, though a good fire has a tendency to go out when you're not looking. Poking it and staring at it during its entire start-up time is part of the ritual for men. In about 30 to 45 minutes it should be ready for cooking.

The fire is perfect when the glow winks saucily from a thin layer of gray-white ash. Spread the coals one layer deep—close together for meaty ribs, thick steaks, or chicken, slightly apart for hot dogs or thin steaks or fish. Add more briquets near the center at this time, if the supply of hot coals is skimpy, and let them burn to glowing coals before you start to cook. If the fire is really good, four or five fresh briquets take only a few minutes to get burning well.

DIRECT OR INDIRECT HEAT?

You can use either direct or indirect heat when you cook over a fire. Food grilled directly over coals cooks faster and you have to be on guard to control

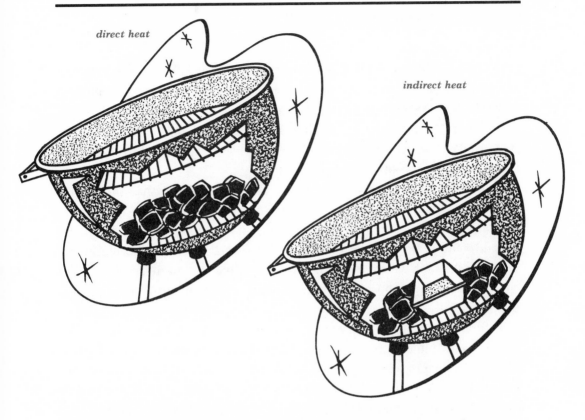

direct heat

indirect heat

flare-ups. For indirect heat, push the coals aside and place a pan in the center; this method is for longer, slower cooking and for particularly fatty foods.

IF YOU BARBECUE WITH GAS

Gas grills start easily. Turn on and light the prime burner, following the manufacturer's instruction to the T for safety's sake. Light the second burner for grilling moderate to large amounts of steak, chicken pieces, or fish, but only one burner may be needed for indirect cooking of brisket or ribs.

Cover the grill and let it heat to cooking temperature, checking the heat indicator that is on most gas grills. When the fire is at proper temperature, add the food and adjust the burner to maintain cooking temperature.

COOKING TECHNIQUES

The proof of a good barbecue cook lies in his or her total immersion in the art of cooking, and enjoying the challenge of getting the fire perfect, food cooked to taste, sauces and seasonings artfully mated to the food. Too much mediocre food gets by because amateur cooks toss it on grills, with little regard for the limitations of cooking the simplest food over a fire in the most basic of cooking equipment.

To understand barbecue cooking, one must realize that the heat is dry, intense, and not easily controlled. Charcoal or wood fires are suitable primarily for prime or choice beef, first-quality tender pork cuts, lamb, and tender poultry. Less tender meats require special handling, marinating, or grinding (as with sausages) to make them edible on a barbecue fire. Thick cuts of meat must be cooked long and slowly to insure thorough heat penetration.

So first, buy top-quality ingredients and the foods best suited to this sort of heat. It makes no sense to skimp on food costs when you must spend a couple of dollars on a bag of charcoal, and much more on wood chips, the grill, and other equipment involved.

Accompanying ingredients—butter, olive and other oils, vinegar, and wines used in cooking—should be of the best quality. This means not necessarily the highest-priced wines, but wines of good flavor to be sure the taste complements the food.

Having acquired fine ingredients, treat them with respect. Barbecuing requires patience, careful watching, and an educated eye, nose, and touch for the doneness of foods.

Meat is seared over a hot charcoal fire, then moved to a less hot area of the grill to continue cooking. Fast-cooking meat such as steak usually is done by the time a good crust cooks on it—at least for rare-meat fans.

Meat that takes longer than 15 minutes to cook benefits from finishing under the cover of a grill or covered by a loose drape of aluminum foil. The foil is tucked loosely around the meat to hold in the heat—not underneath, as that would deter heat penetration. Pull away the foil or cover from time to time, and baste and turn the meat as needed.

A lightweight cover can be constructed of coathanger wires and foil for an open brazier. Bend and fasten the wires into a four-rib umbrella-like frame with a round base and cover it with foil. A vent at the peak of the dome allows heat circulation and serves as a simple damper which you can pinch closed or open wider, according to the needs of the fire or (pinched closed) when you want to intensify smoke flavor. Heat on a grill is controlled by raising or lowering the grill or firebox. If neither grill nor firebox is movable, regulate heat by spreading the coals for a medium heat, pushing them closer together for a hotter fire.

For long-cooking foods, you may need to replenish the fire from time to time with more charcoal briquets. When grilling a turkey or other large piece of meat, I build a fire in a smaller grill set close to the main cooking grill. As more coals are needed, I lift a few with tongs from the auxiliary fire, which keeps the main fire going steadily.

Turn meat as needed to keep dripping fat from blazing and to keep heat even. Don't let the top side of a piece of meat get cold before you turn it to the fire again. About every 10 minutes is sufficient turning for most foods, and half-chickens can be turned only every 20 minutes if you keep the fire low enough to prevent burning. Don't use sauces too often or too heavily. A light brushing with sauce each time you turn meat usually is sufficient. Sauces containing large amounts of oil or other fats, sugar, or tomato should be used very sparingly as they feed the fire and make it jump furiously to char meat. Experienced barbecue cooks use these flammable sauces only in the last 10 to 15 minutes of cooking.

Cooking times are unpredictable due to the variables of wind, fire heat, and chef's diligence. A fuss-budget cook can prolong cooking by basting and turning meat so frequently that it never really heats to cooking temperature. On the other hand, if you let meat stand in one position too long, it overcooks on one side and is half done on the other.

Barbecue is a matter of taste. If you appreciate well-cooked food, you'll soon learn to smell, feel, and taste when barbecue is cooked perfectly. My preference is for meat that is well-browned, crusty and crispy, well-seasoned with sauce, and moist all the way through. Some friends like it dry and crackly all the way through. Each to his own liking, and if you half try, you'll find your way.

SAFETY–IS BARBECUE GOOD FOR YOU?

After publication of the predecessor to this book, *Barbecued Ribs and Other Great Feeds* in 1985, I was asked regularly, "Is barbecue safe?"

A dozen food scientists I asked pooh-poohed the study that suggested carbonized fats as a cancer risk. "I'd never get cancer from the amount of barbecue that I can eat," said Fred Stare of Harvard University. "We barbecue two or three times a week," said my friend Bernie Schweigert of the University of California, Davis, "and my family is in no more danger of early cancer than people who cook by other methods daily."

But tummy aches and more serious illness from poorly handled food are a real hazard of barbecuing; however, they are easily preventable. Marinate fish, poultry, or meat at room temperature no longer than 30 minutes. For longer marinating, be sure to refrigerate it.

Food that is precooked or finished in the oven after grilling or smoking must be cooked continuously. Lag time, when meat can cool to a comfy temperature for growth of harmful bacteria, can spoil the fun. Make the path from kitchen to grill and back fast.

Follow general kitchen sanitation rules at the grill, where slipups can be more dangerous, with many hands in the pot. Wash raw foods and provide covers for salads, desserts, or other uncooked foods. And keep food refrigerated until ready to cook it, hot on the grill, then serve it promptly or refrigerate it.

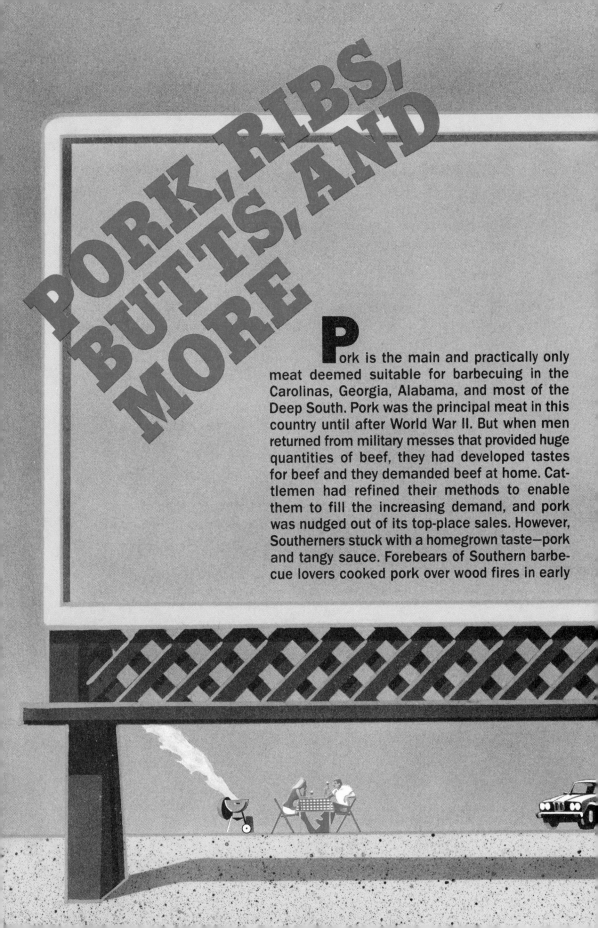

PORK, RIBS, BUTTS, AND MORE

Pork is the main and practically only meat deemed suitable for barbecuing in the Carolinas, Georgia, Alabama, and most of the Deep South. Pork was the principal meat in this country until after World War II. But when men returned from military messes that provided huge quantities of beef, they had developed tastes for beef and they demanded beef at home. Cattlemen had refined their methods to enable them to fill the increasing demand, and pork was nudged out of its top-place sales. However, Southerners stuck with a homegrown taste—pork and tangy sauce. Forebears of Southern barbecue lovers cooked pork over wood fires in early

Colonial times. Legendary Southern hospitality was more likely to entail barbecuing a whole piglet over a pit than sipping tea from dainty cups.

Pork was the meat of the region from white men's earliest explorations. The Spanish explorer DeSoto brought hogs to Florida and Alabama about 1540 and colonizers of Jamestown in 1607 brought swine. The Spanish hogs survived wild in woods where cattle could not survive. Before the Civil War, farmers had domesticated the hogs. The climate was favorable and hogs demanded little time away from the main crops, cotton and tobacco. Pork was plentiful.

The urgency to cook a whole pig once it is butchered no longer exists, thanks to refrigeration. Huge barbecues that took place on plantations where slaves cooked and did other work have given way to more casual Southern hospitality. Host and hostess without servants barbecue less massive cuts of pork. Ribs, pork butts, chops, loins, and meaty tenderloins are barbecued, and occasionally a thick ham steak or chunk of fresh ham. Pig pickin's are left to churches, political rallies, contests, and catered affairs, rather than homes. Traditional barbecue still is cooked at modest restaurants throughout the Southeast. You are served sliced or shredded meat, Brunswick stew, coleslaw, and hushpuppies at a table covered in oilcloth.

Savor good barbecue in Wilson, Chapel Hill, or Rocky Mount, North Carolina, or countless spots in the South. But don't feel deprived with ribs as a main item. Nothing tastes finer when they're barbecued brown and tangy. Ribs are country-style when I want more meat than fun, but I buy spareribs or baby back ribs for crispy, finger-lickin' eating.

I was happy to find a snowy-headed man at a church in Coconut Grove, Florida, barbecuing ribs a couple of years ago. It used to be a Saturday ritual buying ribs at this same spot from women who grilled them over tiny fires in washtubs in the fifties and sixties. Now the old man does his bit for the church, and is as secretive about the sauce as the women were 30 years earlier.

Barbecue as it is practiced in the South owes much to the fine taste for spice and seasonings that Africans brought to this country. Much of the best barbecue in this country is done by blacks, at churches, in commercial establishments, and as caterers.

Pork barbecue in California is full of the tastes of the Orient. Chinese barbecued ribs or pork roast appeal to the American palate. Hispanics are adding their flavors. Pork was a major meat in the Caribbean as long as it was in North America.

Nowadays rib places are anywhere in the country. In New York you'll find meat that has been cooked in Texas or New Jersey and shipped to the restaurant, where the ribs are swabbed simply with sauce and heated. Some are good, but not like a mess of ribs grilled right at home, the fragrance stimulating our appetites to almost painful hunger. Then the first bite. That's ribs!

BARBECUED RIBS

There are three types of ribs—spareribs, that are cut from just behind the pork shoulder; back ribs; and country-style ribs, cut from the loin. America's favorite is spareribs, an elongated triangle of bones, cartilage, and a thin layer of meat that grills to a crispiness and flavor like no other food. Back ribs are shorter than spareribs, and so make daintier finger food and are preferred for Chinese-style ribs. Country-style ribs have nuggets of meat attached to bones. They cook tender and juicy, with crispy edges.

Any kind of ribs can be cooked by the methods here. Individual recipes call for certain sauces, but use a good commercial one or another sauce to suit your taste. You can start a lively argument over sauces. I like most of them, but have my favorites, too. The choice varies from the thin, vinegary and peppery concoctions of the Carolinas to thick catsupy sauces of Kansas City and lime-juice and catsup sauces of Florida. Barbecue rubs, a mix of salt and seasonings, goes on ribs in Texas, and sauce just at the end. A different sauce may be served at table.

These are the major cooking methods for home grills.

GRILL AND BASTE, OPEN FIRE

Ribs in large pieces (a side if they are spareribs) are easier to turn and baste than cut ribs. Carve them into two- or three-rib portions after they are cooked. Or if you are doing small cuts of ribs put several of them in a wire basket for barbecuing, so you can turn the basket, rather than individual pieces. When the fire flares up a chef is grateful for ribs or a basketful that he can turn or pull off the grill in one motion. Fast work helps the cook to quench the flames and keep sooty smoke from ruining the ribs.

If the grill height is adjustable, set the rack 8 to 10 inches above hot coals. For a one-level grill, build the fire small—only one layer of charcoal— and have charcoal ready to replenish the fire. Poke in a few briquets at a time to keep the fire burning slowly but steadily. Rub ribs with a seasoning mixture or brush a vinegar or bone-broth sauce on them before starting. Sweet or fatty sauces or those containing catsup should be reserved for the final few minutes of cooking. (See Luther's Barbecued Ribs.)

Start the fire early enough so that it burns down to glowing coals covered with gray ash. Place the ribs on the grill rack. Keep an eye on them and turn them each time flames leap up. Baste occasionally with whatever sauce is called for in the recipes, or if using a sauce of your choice, baste during the first 20 minutes with light sauces. Continue to turn and baste ribs every 10 minutes or each time fire flares. After 20 minutes, start basting lightly with sweet or fatty sauces. Total cooking time will be 45 minutes to 1 hour. Ribs should be a rich brown color, but not charred or sooty. Make a cut near the center between two bones. If the juices are pink, return the ribs to the grill and continue cooking until juices run clear. When no pink shows, the ribs are done. They can be kept hot in a large dish covered with foil and set at the side of the grill, if you want to delay serving them. Or cut in 2- or 3-rib portions, using kitchen shears or a sharp knife, and serve immediately with more sauce or a table sauce.

GRILL AND BASTE, CLOSED GRILL

Place the ribs on the grill 5 to 6 inches above a fire that has burned down to glowing coals covered with gray ash. Baste with a vinegar or bone-broth sauce, but not sweet or fatty sauce. Brown on one side, turn and brown on other side. Baste ribs lightly with a sweet or fatty sauce or heavily with vinegar or bone-broth sauce, cover grill, and adjust dampers and vents to prevent fire flare-ups. Cook, turning and basting lightly every 10 to 12 minutes, about 45 minutes total, until crispy and done.

Uncover grill, brush ribs again with sauce, turn, and grill 2 or 3 minutes. Remove to a platter, cut in 2- or 3-rib portions, using kitchen shears or a sharp knife, and serve with more sauce or table sauce, as desired.

LUTHER'S BARBECUED RIBS

My husband preferred barbecued ribs to almost any other food, and he must have barbecued two to three thousand pounds of them this way in his lifetime.
The sauce for this recipe circulated first around north Florida, then Miami barbecue grills for years. Luther's rule was limes for ribs, lemon in the sauce for chicken. At various times, we plucked the limes off our back yard tree.

4 to 5 pounds spareribs
Florida Barbecue Sauce (page 192)

Makes 4 to 6 servings.

Place ribs about 6 inches above hot coals. Brush lightly with sauce and brown on one side. Keep a water bottle handy when using this sauce as it causes flames to shoot up. Turn, brush again with sauce, and brown the other side. Continue turning and basting about every 10 minutes until ribs are done, about 1 hour. Check by cutting near bone in a center section. If juices run clear or golden the ribs are done. Remove ribs to a platter. Cut into 1- to 3-rib sections with scissors or a sharp knife and serve with any remaining sauce.

BARBECUED RIBS WITH SALSA

4 to 5 pounds country-style ribs
Dry Rub for Ribs (page 189)
1 small onion, chopped
1 clove garlic, minced
1 tablespoon oil
1 (8-ounce) can tomato sauce
2 to 4 tablespoons chopped green chiles (canned or roasted fresh)
Salt to taste

Makes 4 to 6 servings.

Sprinkle ribs with seasoning mix and place 4 to 6 inches above hot coals. Grill about 45 minutes, turning as needed to cook evenly and extinguishing any flames with squirts of water.

Meanwhile, in a saucepan over moderate heat cook onion and garlic in oil until tender but not browned. Add tomato sauce and bring to a boil. Remove from heat and add chiles. Taste and add salt, if needed. When ribs are done brush lightly with the sauce (salsa) and cook a minute or two longer. Remove ribs to platter; cut into serving-size sections, using scissors or a sharp knife. Serve salsa on the side.

PEPPERY BARBECUED RIBS

1 medium onion, diced

1 rib celery, diced, to make 1/2 cup

2 tablespoons oil

2 cloves garlic, minced

1 cup catsup

1/2 cup water

2 tablespoons cider vinegar

1 teaspoon freshly ground black pepper

1 teaspoon crushed red pepper

4 to 5 pounds country-style ribs

2 teaspoons Dry Rub for Ribs (page 189)

Makes 4 to 6 servings.

In an enamelware or stainless-steel saucepan sauté onion and celery in oil until almost tender. Add garlic and sauté 2 or 3 minutes longer. Add catsup, water, vinegar, and the peppers. Simmer uncovered 15 minutes to blend flavors. Stir occasionally and add more water if sauce thickens too much.

Sprinkle ribs generously with seasoning mix. Grill 4 to 5 inches over hot fire, turning often, until browned and almost done, about 40 minutes. Brush lightly with sauce and turn and grill until browned and done, about 15 minutes longer. Heat and serve remaining sauce with the ribs at table.

DIXIE BARBECUED RIBS

Ribs *finished with a sauce sweetened with catsup and seasoned with mustard and garlic is tops for summer weekends in thousands of Southern gardens. Moistening with pepper water keeps meat juicy and prevents charring.*

2 cups water

½ teaspoon crushed red pepper or 2 or 3
    dried red chiles

4 to 5 pounds spareribs or country-style ribs

Georgia Barbecue Sauce (page 193)

Makes 4 servings.

Combine water and red pepper in saucepan. Heat on grill and keep hot at edge. Trim surface fat from ribs. Place sides of ribs on rack 8 to 10 inches above glowing coals or use small fire if rack cannot be adjusted. Heat ribs on both sides until surface is warm and brush with pepper water. Cover grill or make a tent with aluminum foil. Continue barbecuing and brushing with pepper water for 30 minutes. Brush lightly with Georgia Barbecue Sauce, turn, and brush lightly with sauce. Continue barbecuing 15 to 30 minutes, until juices run clear when ribs are cut near center. Turn every 10 minutes or each time fire flares and brush lightly with sauce. Heat remaining sauce. Cut ribs into serving pieces and serve with sauce.

TEXAS BARBECUED RIBS

In spite of their noted preference for beef at ranch barbecues, the late Walter Jeffords, barbecue chef to President and Lady Byrd Johnson, barbecued thousands of pounds of pork ribs in a method similar to this in his lifetime as a barbecue caterer.

4 to 5 pounds spareribs

Dry Rub for Ribs (page 189)

Bone-Broth Basting Sauce (page 195)

Texas Barbecue Sauce (page 194)

Makes
4 to 5
servings.

Sprinkle ribs generously with seasoning mix, rubbing some of it under the flap of meat on the bony side of each slab of ribs. Brush well with bone-broth sauce and place ribs 4 to 5 inches above hot fire on grill with a cover. Brown on one side, baste, and turn. Brown well. Cover grill, adjust dampers so fire burns slowly, and grill ribs until done, about 45 minutes. While cooking, turn and baste four or five times, lifting cover only as needed so grill stays hot. Ribs are done if juices run clear with no trace of pink when meat between ribs is slit near center. Remove cover, brush ribs again, and remove to platter. Carve in 1- or 2-rib portions and serve with Texas Barbecue Sauce and coleslaw.

PIG PICKIN'S, HOME–STYLE

Pork butts instead of whole hogs are a usual weekend barbecue in the Carolinas. They are grilled slowly, water-smoked (page 164), or simmered a long time in a kettle or slow cooker. A pork butt looks large, but after skin, bones, and fat are discarded, it is cut down to family size. Grill two or more for a crowd.

1 Boston butt, about 5 pounds
Carolina Barbecue Sauce (Eastern, Piedmont,
   or Western, page 190)

*Makes 10
servings.*

Trim surface fat on meat to a thin layer. Build fire 45 minutes before cooking and let burn down to low coals. Spread coals and place drip pan in firebox. Oil grill or spritz with nonstick spray. Place pork over drip pan and cook by indirect heat for 3 to 4 hours, or until 160 degrees on meat thermometer. Cool meat. Pull meat from skin, bones, and fat. Chop and mix with sauce just to moisten. Serve on buns or on plate. Serve more sauce on the side.

PIG PICKIN'S

North Carolina pig pickin's have brought several thousand dollars to CAREF, the foundation of the International Association of Cooking Professionals that provides scholarships to aspiring wine and food students.

Merle Ellis, author of the syndicated column The Butcher from Marin County, California, offers a pig pickin' anywhere in the United States for the CAREF benefit auction. One engagement alone raised more than $3,000 from 25 guests on Long Island.

A traditional pig-pickin' is centered around hogs weighing 80 to 100 pounds barbecued on cookers large enough to tow on boat trailers. Ellis simplifies the procedure, and grills Boston butts on a kettle grill, keeping the heat low by adding moist hickory chips throughout the six hours of cooking.

The menu is as authentic as if it were in Wake County or Chatham County, North Carolina. There are traditional Brunswick stew, Piedmont-style coleslaw (white), potato salad, hushpuppies, and shredded meat on buns. Ellis takes his wife along to help, but he shreds the coleslaw, as any butcher knows knife work, and he inveigles the host or hostess and volunteers to lend a hand.

BARBECUED PORK BUTT

Whole hog was the original, but commercial barbecuers and homefolk choose butts these days. Ask your meat person to bone and tie the butt to make it easier to carve. Backyard cooks barbecue two or three butts for a big party.

1 pork butt, boned and tied, 6 to 7 pounds
Basic Dry Rub (page 189)
Barbecue sauce (Carolina, Georgia, or Florida are
    typical, but almost any sauce is good)
Hickory or mesquite chips, soaked
Sandwich buns, split, toasted and buttered

Makes 10 to 12 servings.

A grill with cover is almost essential to this cut of meat to ensure slow, even heat. When fire is burned down to hot coals covered with gray ash, push coals to the back or sides and place a drip pan in place. If barbecuing more than one butt, provide drip pan for each or large drip pan to catch drips from all. Coat meat with dry rub and place over drip pan. Cover grill and cook 30 minutes. Spritz out flames if they occur.

Working quickly so as not to lose heat, turn pork to help even browning, brush lightly with sauce, and close cover again. Turn and baste meat every 20 to 30 minutes. Keep fire moderate, adding a few lighted briquets from another grill to keep it steady. Barbecue pork 5 hours, until it almost falls apart. Add hickory or mesquite chips to fire after 4½ hours.

Shred meat into bowl, using fingers, fork, and small knife. Mix in 1 cup sauce. Serve in buns with more sauce.

GLAZED COUNTRY RIBS

4 to 5 pounds country-style ribs
Dry Rub for Ribs (page 189)
Bone-Broth Basting Sauce (page 195)
2 tablespoons cornstarch
1/4 cup packed brown sugar
1 1/2 cups pineapple juice
1/4 cup prepared horseradish
2 tablespoons cider vinegar
Freshly grated horseradish, if available

Makes
5 to 6
servings.

Rub ribs with seasoning mix. Place on grill 6 to 8 inches above hot coals, brush with bone-broth sauce, and grill until browned. Turn and brown the other side. Continue grilling, turning and basting, until ribs are almost done, about 45 minutes.

Meanwhile, in a small saucepan blend cornstarch and brown sugar. Stir in pineapple juice until smooth. Bring to a boil at edge of grill, stirring constantly, and cook and stir until thickened and clear. Stir in horseradish and vinegar. Keep glaze warm. Brush glaze on ribs and cook and turn until they are shiny. Remove ribs to platter and cut into serving-size sections, using scissors or a sharp knife. Serve remaining glaze with ribs.

CALIFORNIA PORK CHOP BARBECUE

After a long hot drive on a summer weekend, we often used to stop at Love's Barbecue near Los Angeles for a barbecued pork sandwich instead of going home to cook supper. We adored the barbecue, and I was amazed to discover that liquid smoke flavoring was the secret of the heady flavor, though smoke poured from what I thought was the barbecue hut. Commercially prepared smoke flavor is a pure distillate of hickory smoke, but use it with discretion or the concentrated flavor takes on a medicinal taste. I like only a teaspoonful in this sauce.

6 pork chops, 1 inch thick

1½ cups catsup

¼ cup soy sauce

1 to 2 teaspoons liquid smoke

2 tablespoons vinegar

Makes 6 servings.

Grill chops 4 to 6 inches above hot coals, turning to cook evenly, until done but not dry. This will take about 30 minutes.

Meanwhile, in a small saucepan at edge of grill combine catsup, soy sauce, liquid smoke, and vinegar. Stir and heat until well blended. Brush hot sauce on chops and glaze for about 5 minutes over coals. Remove meat to platter and serve with remaining sauce at table.

CAROLINA BARBECUED PORK CHOPS

Meaty center-cut loin chops are sumptuous for this barbecue, but loin end or shoulder chops can be used. Chops cut about an inch thick give you juicy meat.

6 center-cut loin pork chops, 1 inch thick

Carolina Barbecue Sauce (page 190)

Applesauce or Raisinberry Sauce (page 202)

Makes 6 servings.

Dip chops in basting sauce and place on grill 4 to 6 inches above hot coals. Grill until browned, then turn, baste, and grill on other side until browned. Move to edge of grill and grill until done as desired, turning and basting as necessary to cook evenly and prevent flare-ups. Total cooking time for 1-inch chops will be about 35 minutes. Remove to hot platter and serve with applesauce or Raisinberry Sauce.

GRILLED PORK STEAKS

In my market pork steaks are cut about 1/2 inch thick, so I order ahead and get the butcher to cut me 3/4-inch steaks in order to have the meaty thickness that makes this barbecue juicier and more succulent. Pork steaks are cut from the shoulder.

4 pork steaks, 3/4 inch thick

1/4 cup beef or chicken broth

1/4 cup dry white wine

1 tablespoon minced fresh or 1/2 teaspoon dried rosemary

1 tablespoon minced fresh or 1/2 teaspoon dried
        marjoram

1 clove garlic, smashed

1/2 teaspoon salt

2 tablespoons oil

*Makes 4
servings.*

Trim as much fat as possible off edges of pork steaks. Place meat in a plastic bag. Combine broth, wine, herbs, garlic, and salt. Add to pork, close bag tightly, and place in dish. Marinate in refrigerator several hours or overnight. Drain pork, reserving marinade.

Grill 4 to 6 inches above medium-hot coals, brushing with marinade now and then and turning to cook evenly. In about 30 minutes, pork should be fully cooked but juicy. Brush with oil and remaining marinade. Serve hot.

SAGE PORK TENDERLOIN

A *clump of sage flourished in an herb bed a few feet from our barbecue grill in Encino, California, so putting a few sprigs of sage on a roast came naturally. If you don't have fresh sage, sprinkle the meat with a couple teaspoons of dried leaf sage.*

1 pork tenderloin, about 1½ pounds
4 to 5 sprigs fresh sage
Salt and freshly ground pepper
Olive oil

Makes 6 to 8 servings.

Slit pork almost through to open out like a book. Place sage in the cavity and sprinkle lightly with salt and pepper. Tie pork into its original shape.

Grill 3 to 4 inches from hot fire until browned, turning to cook evenly. Move to edge of grill and brush with oil. Cover grill or tuck a loose tent of foil around pork to hold in heat. Continue to cook until meat thermometer inserted in center registers 160 degrees, about 35 minutes longer. A few sprigs of fresh sage may be thrown on the fire a few minutes before removing meat from grill. Carve meat in thin slices on board or platter and serve with Sage Butter (page 205), if desired.

PORK RIBS WITH RAISINBERRY SAUCE

This sauce gives a holidaylike flair to ribs, and you'll think of it for chicken and turkey, too.

4 to 6 pounds spareribs, country-style ribs,
     or back ribs
Dry Rub for Ribs (page 189)
Raisinberry Sauce (page 202)

Makes
4 to 6
servings.

Trim excess surface fat from ribs and sprinkle meat with seasoning mix. Let stand at room temperature about 30 minutes.

Arrange a drip pan at one side or end of grill and push hot coals to back of grill or arrange them around drip pan. Place ribs about 6 inches over hot coals, bone side down, and grill until lightly browned. Turn and brown other side. Move ribs over drip pan, then cover grill or drape a tent of foil loosely over ribs to hold in heat. Cook, turning ribs every 15 minutes, until ribs are done but not charred, about 1 hour. Turn ribs meat side up, drizzle with Raisinberry Sauce, and heat 2 or 3 minutes. Remove ribs to platter; cut into serving-size sections. Serve remaining sauce with ribs.

GINGERED PORK TENDERLOIN

This lean, tender cut of pork is becoming increasingly available due to new cut styles in large pork packing houses. The tenderloin is a favorite of the Chinese and benefits from Oriental-style seasonings, as in this treatment.

1 pork tenderloin, about 1½ pounds

2 cloves garlic, minced

4 thin slices fresh ginger root, or ½ teaspoon
     ground ginger

⅓ cup soy sauce

2 tablespoons sugar

2 tablespoons water

1 tablespoon oil

Makes 6 servings, sliced very thin.

If meat is more than 2½ inches thick, split it into 2 long strips. Place in plastic bag. In a cup combine garlic, ginger, soy sauce, sugar, water, and oil. Pour over meat, close bag tightly, and turn to coat meat well. Place bag in bowl and let meat marinate at room temperature 1 hour or in the refrigerator 3 to 4 hours, turning bag 2 or 3 times. Carefully drain marinade into a small saucepan.

Using a drip pan, cook meat over hot coals, turning to cook evenly, until browned. Move to edge of grill over drip pan; close cover or cover meat loosely with a tent of foil to hold in heat. Grill, turning meat now and then and brushing with marinade about every 5 minutes. Total cooking time will be about 45 minutes. Slice very thin and serve warm with hot mustard or chutney.

Note: This tenderloin can also be served at room temperature or well chilled, so any leftovers are welcome. Thin-sliced pork with a cold noodle salad makes a grand lunch the next day.

CHINESE–STYLE BARBECUED PORK

I was a young woman in Miami when I first had what my date called Chinese roast pork with hot and heavenly sauce. This is my adaptation, after I learned that the restaurateur's "hot and heavenly" is American catsup and mustard.

1/4 cup sweet sherry

1/3 cup soy sauce

1 tablespoon sugar

1 tablespoon grated fresh ginger root

1 clove garlic, minced

1 boneless pork rib end roast, 2 1/2 pounds

1/3 cup catsup

1 tablespoon dry mustard

2 to 3 teaspoons water

Makes

6 to 8

generous

servings.

Combine sherry, soy sauce, sugar, ginger, and garlic. Mix well. Place pork in a dish or plastic bag, add sauce, and brush over meat or close bag tightly and turn to coat meat with sauce. Marinate at room temperature 1 hour or in the refrigerator overnight.

This cut of pork is best cooked on a grill with a cover or on a spit. If you do not have a spit or grill with a cover, shape a loose tent of foil over the meat to hold in heat and help prevent flare-ups while cooking.

Remove meat from marinade, reserving marinade, and place on grill 6 to 8 inches above a drip pan surrounded by hot coals or with coals pushed to the back of the grill. Brush meat with sauce and grill 1 hour, basting and turning as needed to cook evenly and prevent flare-ups. Test with a meat thermometer. When internal temperature reaches 160 degrees, meat is thoroughly cooked but still tender and juicy. A thick roast might require 30 minutes longer.

Just before meat is done, mix catsup into remaining marinade and brush over meat. Turn and glaze meat over drip pan. Remove meat to a platter, cover loosely with foil, and let stand 30 minutes. About 10 minutes before serving, mix dry mustard to a smooth thin paste with water. Thinly slice the pork. Serve catsup sauce and mustard sauce separately, or swirl the mustard into the catsup sauce.

PORK AND APPLES

This is an Indian summer dish, good after the best fall apples come to market.

4 pork loin chops, 1 inch thick, about 2 pounds total

1 cup apple juice

2 tablespoons lemon juice

1 teaspoon leaf sage

2 tablespoons brown sugar

1 onion, minced

2 to 3 firm apples (Greening, Ida Red, Granny Smith)

Salt and freshly ground pepper

Makes 4 servings.

Place meat in a plastic bag. In a small bowl mix apple and lemon juices, sage, brown sugar, and onion and stir until sugar is dissolved. Pour over meat. Close bag tightly and turn to coat chops well with the marinade. Place in a bowl and refrigerate several hours or overnight. Remove chops from marinade and drain well.

Grill over hot coals for 20 minutes, turning and basting with marinade now and then. Core apples but do not peel. Cut in thick rings. Brush apples with marinade and place on grill around pork. Continue grilling pork and apples until pork is done as desired and apples are tender, about 15 minutes. Remove from grill and sprinkle lightly with salt and pepper.

Note: To prepare this combination when good cooking apples are unavailable, open a can of pie-sliced apples (not pie filling) and heat in a skillet with a few bits of pork fat trimmings, a slice or two of onion, and a dash of lemon juice. Serve hot with pork.

DEVILED PORK CUBES

1 to 1¼ pounds boneless pork loin, 1 inch thick
4 thick slices bacon
2 to 3 tablespoons Dijon-style mustard
½ cup fine dry bread crumbs (see Note)
1 tablespoon minced parsley or cilantro (fresh coriander
    leaves)

Makes 4 servings.

Cut pork into 1-inch cubes. Cut bacon in 1-inch squares. Next, prepare 4 skewers, each of which will hold about 7 cubes of pork and 8 bacon squares. Thread bacon and pork on skewers, starting with bacon, alternating, and ending with bacon. Meat and bacon should not be jammed on but pushed together firmly. Spread a spoonful of mustard on a plate or square of waxed paper and roll each pork skewer in it. Mix bread crumbs with parsley or cilantro on another plate or square of paper. Roll each skewer in this mixture. Skewers can be prepared ahead of time and refrigerated before cooking.

Grill over hot coals, turning to brown evenly. Pork will be juicy and tender but thoroughly cooked in about 20 minutes. Push pork off onto plates with a fork.

Note: I keep fine dry bread crumbs in my freezer. When good French bread dries out, as it often does with the uneven schedule of today's eating, I process it in a blender or with the shredding blade of a food processor. Then I package it in a covered freezer container or bag, and have it ready to go at a moment's notice.

LEMON–GLAZED PORK LOIN

1 boned and tied pork loin, 3½ to 4 pounds

½ cup lemon juice

¼ cup oil

¼ cup soy sauce

2 tablespoons brown sugar

1 tablespoon Dijon-style mustard

Makes 6 servings, with leftovers.

Place drip pan in firebox of grill, pushing hot coals to the back or around drip pan. Place meat over drip pan and grill until browned, turning as needed to cook evenly. Cover grill and adjust dampers so that fire burns slowly. If grill has no cover, place a loose tent of foil over roast to hold in heat.

Meanwhile, mix together lemon juice, oil, soy sauce, brown sugar, and mustard. Beat well to blend. Brush on meat several times while grilling. After 1½ hours test with a meat thermometer. Continue basting and turning meat until internal temperature registers 160 degrees on thermometer. Remove to platter and let stand 20 minutes before carving.

This is good with sweet potatoes roasted on the grill or, in summer, fresh corn on the cob.

SPITTED PORK WITH ORANGE SAUCE

This sauce can be used on lamb, ham, or turkey as well as pork. Orange and smoke flavors are highly regarded by barbecue cooks in Florida. We have used this sauce to barbecue fresh red snapper, too, with fine results.

1 pork loin or boned and tied loin roast, 4 to 5 pounds

1 cup orange juice

1/2 cup lemon juice

2 tablespoons soy sauce

1 clove garlic, minced

1/2 teaspoon ground cloves

1/3 cup sugar

1 tablespoon cornstarch

1/2 teaspoon cinnamon

1 tablespoon grated orange peel

4 orange slices with peel, halved

Makes 5 to 6 servings.

If using pork with bone, have the butcher crack the backbone for easier carving. Place pork in plastic bag. Mix orange and lemon juices, soy sauce, garlic, and cloves. Pour into bag with pork, close bag tightly, and turn to coat meat with sauce. Place bag in bowl and refrigerate overnight, turning now and then. Remove meat from bag and reserve marinade.

Place meat on spit, making sure it is balanced to turn smoothly, and fasten with spit forks. Engage spit so meat turns about 6 inches above hot coals. Roast meat until meat thermometer registers 160 degrees, about 1 1/2 hours. Remove pork from spit and let stand on board or platter 20 to 30 minutes before carving.

Meanwhile, in a small saucepan mix sugar, cornstarch, cinnamon, and orange peel. Add reserved marinade and cook and stir over medium heat until thickened and translucent, about 5 minutes. Add orange slices to heat through. Serve hot with carved meat.

BARBECUED HAM
AND HONEYED PINEAPPLE

*T*his *makes a handsome and easy patio supper if you use ham labeled fully cooked, which needs only thorough heating to develop the flavor (see Note).*

1 steak cut from a fully cooked whole or semiboneless
     ham, 2 inches thick
1/2 cup unsweetened pineapple juice
2 tablespoons oil
1 teaspoon prepared mustard, plus 1/4 cup for sauce
1 large ripe pineapple
About 2 tablespoons honey

*Makes
6 to 8
servings.*

If you are unable to get a thick ham steak, cut your own from a fully cooked ham roll, canned ham, cooked country-cured ham, or a home-baked ham. You will need a meat saw for a ham with bone.

Slash the fat edges of the ham to prevent curling. Place ham in a shallow dish. Beat together pineapple juice, oil, and 1 teaspoon mustard. Pour over ham and marinate at room temperature 1 to 2 hours.

Trim any long lethal spikes off pineapple crown and discard any dried spikes. With a very sharp, heavy knife cut pineapple into 6 or 8 lengthwise wedges. Trim crown for neatness but leave core intact to retain shape of pineapple. Place fruit on a long platter and drizzle with honey. Let stand 1 to 2 hours.

Place ham about 6 inches above hot coals. Brush with marinade. Grill 15 minutes or until browned. Turn and brush with marinade. Arrange pineapple in circle around ham on grill. Turn pineapple often as it tends to burn fast. Cook ham 15 minutes longer and grill pineapple until heated through and tinged with brown. Place ham on warm platter and surround with pineapple. For sauce, mix remaining pineapple marinade with 1/4 cup mustard or thin mustard with pineapple juice to serve as sauce. Slice to serve.

Note: Country ham can be used in this grill supper if you treat it first to prevent its drying out. Have the butcher cut a thick steak from the center (the ends of a whole ham will be ready for boiling and glazing to serve another time). Pour hot water over the thick ham slice and let it stand 2 to 3 hours to moisten the meat and soak out some of the salt. Marinate ham as directed above; then remove from marinade and grill.

KEY WEST ROAST PIG

The holiday aroma of Key West and the Cuban quarter of Miami is that of roasting pig, a tradition of the refugees and cigar workers who live in Key West. This recipe's method is adapted from a fine Key West cook. The first trick is to persuade a butcher that you want an infant pig. Although specialty butchers now cater to the demand for small animals for barbecuing, we have been stuck with pigs as large as 29 pounds. Nonetheless, even the large ones make gustatory events.

1 baby pig, preferably 12 to 18 pounds

4 to 6 sour oranges (much preferred) or limes

About 1 tablespoon dried oregano

3 to 4 cloves garlic, minced

Butter

Watercress, parsley, or other greens, for garnish

Limes, other small citrus (calamondins, tangerines, or lemons) or olives, for garnish

Makes 8 to 12 company servings, with leftover pickings.

Order a pig well in advance, begging for a small one so it will rest full-length on the grill. Otherwise, have the pig cut crosswise in half to grill it, then reassemble it for serving. Clear a shelf in the refrigerator.

Have the pig thoroughly cleaned. A few remaining bristles can be pulled out with tweezers or a strawberry huller, or shave bristles with a clean disposable razor. Cut tendons in inside knee joints, front and back, so legs can be folded under pig.

Cut sour oranges (more aromatic than any other citrus) or limes and squeeze generously over and inside pig, rubbing juice into skin and cavity. Rub with oregano and garlic. Leave some of the cut citrus in the cavity. Place the pig in a large bag such as a tall kitchen garbage bag, close with a twist tie, and refrigerate overnight.

About 5½ hours before serving, start fire in grill and let coals burn down. The fire must be replenished periodically while cooking, so a portable grill to supply fresh burning coals should be set up nearby.

Remove pig from bag and skewer or sew the cavity closed, shaping body as roundly as possible. Rub the pig thoroughly with soft butter. Place a lime in the mouth to prop jaws open evenly, as this is the shape that the mouth will take. Skewer legs to the pig in folded position.

Place pig about 10 inches above hot coals, positioning it back side up first. Turn from side to side and back side down, brushing with more butter to keep moist. If ears and snout brown too rapidly, cover with folds of foil to prevent burning, though the crisp ears are delicacies. Add coals as needed to keep fire burning steadily but not flaming.

After 3 to 3½ hours, insert a meat thermometer in an inside joint, being careful not to touch bone. When the thermometer shows an internal temperature of 160 to 165 degrees, pig is done. This may take up to 5 hours total on an uncovered grill or as little as 3 hours on a covered grill. Place pig on a platter; remove strings and skewers and the cooked lime from the mouth. Push a fresh lime in place. Garnish extravagantly with watercress or other greens, placing a ringlet around the neck and, if the pig was cut to fit the grill, a wide sash around the center to cover the cut. Skewer a slice of lime or an olive to each eye.

To carve, cut down the backbone and cut off chops. Cut away legs and carve them into thin slices. The head, ears, and small shank portions usually are picked off the bones or crispy bits of skin gnawed blissfully.

SPIT–BARBECUED HAM

1 piece fully cooked boneless ham, 3 pounds
1/2 cup honey
1/2 cup wine vinegar

Makes
8 to 10
servings.

Score the ham with shallow cuts. Place on spit and check to make sure it is balanced. Fasten with spit forks. Push coals to back of firebox and place a drip pan in front. Attach spit so coals are about 4 inches from ham. Engage spit and start motor. Cook ham 40 to 45 minutes, until internal temperature on a meat thermometer reaches 125 degrees.

Beat together honey and vinegar. Brush on ham every 2 or 3 minutes and cook 15 minutes longer. Let sit 10 to 20 minutes before carving.

GINGERY HAM STEAK

4 or 5 thin slices fresh ginger root
1 cup pineapple juice
1/4 cup packed brown sugar
1 center-cut ham steak, 1 1/2 to 2 inches thick
1 tablespoon cornstarch
Water

Makes 6
servings.

In a small saucepan combine ginger root, pineapple juice, and brown sugar. Stir over fire at edge of grill until brown sugar is dissolved. Slash fatty edges of ham to prevent curling.

Place ham 4 to 5 inches above hot coals. Grill until lightly browned, about 15 minutes; turn and brown the other side. Brush with sauce and turn and brown first one, then the other side. This will take about 15 minutes.

Just before removing ham from grill, blend cornstarch with a small amount of water to make a thin smooth paste. Stir into remaining basting sauce and cook and stir until smooth and translucent. If too thick, stir in more pineapple juice or water. Slice ham and serve with sauce.

BREAKFAST SAUSAGE KEBABS

Cook a pot of grits (page 230) or Country-Fried Potatoes (page 242) at the edge of the grill to go with this weekend breakfast. Toast thick slices of French bread, too.

1 small onion, chopped

2 tablespoons oil

1 small clove garlic, minced

1 (8-ounce) can tomato sauce

2 tablespoons brown sugar

2 pounds pork sausage links

2 apples, quartered

2 green peppers, seeded and cut into chunks

Makes 6 servings.

In a small saucepan cook onion in oil until tender but not browned. Add garlic and cook a minute or 2. Stir in tomato sauce and brown sugar. Keep warm while preparing kebabs. Alternate sausage, apples, and green pepper on skewers, spearing sausages crosswise, slightly diagonally. Prick sausages once or twice each.

Grill 6 inches above hot coals, turning and basting with sauce to cook evenly and prevent burning. Serve sausages, apples, and green pepper hot with any remaining sauce as well as buttered grits or Country-Fried Potatoes and toasted French bread.

BARBECUED SAUSAGE

Barbecue guests usually like substantial before-dinner food, and this is perfect — sausage given an extra smoking over your grill and served with sauce. For a light meal, this can be the main dish, with toasted buns and a big bowlful of potato salad.

Smoked, Italian, or big link sausage
Barbecue sauce of your choice (pages 190–203)

Place sausage at edge of grill and heat, turning often. Prick with a fork once or twice to allow excess fat to cook out. When heated through remove to a chopping board, cut in small pieces, spear with picks, and serve with your choice of sauce on the side. If sausage requires cooking, make sure it is thoroughly cooked before serving. Small link sausages can be cooked the same way, but are more difficult to keep track of and require much turning to cook evenly.

POLYNESIAN PORK BURGERS

Old-fashioned ideas of fatty pork no longer hold. Today's pork is so lean that it needs ground beef mixed in to produce a juicy burger.

1½ pounds ground lean pork
½ pound ground lean beef
2 tablespoons soy sauce
½ small green pepper, finely chopped
8 pineapple rings

Makes 8 servings.

Combine pork, beef, soy sauce, and green pepper. Mix lightly but thoroughly. Shape mixture into patties about 1 inch thick.

Grill 4 to 5 inches above hot coals until browned, then turn and brown the other side. Meanwhile, place pineapple rings at edge of grill to warm them. When pork patties are browned, move meat to edge of grill and the pineapple rings to the center. Grill meat and pineapple until done and pineapple begins to brown. Move pineapple rings to tops of pork patties as they brown. Test pork for doneness by cutting into the center of each patty. Juice runs clear or golden, not pink, if pork is done. Serve hot with more soy sauce, if desired.

SAUSAGE AND PEPPERS

This classic Italian-style knife-and-fork sandwich is peddled from pushcarts at the wildly wonderful Feast of San Gennaro each summer in New York's Little Italy. The pushcarts are equipped with miniature steam tables that keep the sausage and peppers hot. Sausage and peppers grilled over charcoal are even better than on the street, to my taste.

2 medium green bell peppers
2 medium red or yellow bell peppers
1 medium onion
2 large cloves garlic, minced
Salt and freshly ground pepper
2 tablespoons olive oil
1½ pounds sweet or hot Italian sausage
2 long loaves Italian bread, split and toasted

Makes 4 to 6 servings.

Remove seeds and spines from peppers and cut peppers in strips or squares. Pile peppers in center of a large rectangle of heavy-duty aluminum foil (or you can cook this in a skillet with a cover). Peel and slice onion and place over peppers. Sprinkle with garlic, salt, black pepper, and oil. Fold foil over vegetables, allowing space for steam but sealing foil package tightly with a double fold. Place at edge of grill in which a hot fire is ready for cooking.

If it is in 1 piece, cut sausage in 3- or 4-inch lengths. Grill sausage over hot coals, browning on all sides while you turn meat and squirt any leaping flames with water to prevent burning. This will take 15 to 18 minutes. When sausages are browned, unwrap or uncover vegetables, protecting hands with a barbecue mitt. Place sausages over pepper mixture and seal packet again. Move to a hotter section of grill and cook until sausages are done through and peppers tender, 10 to 15 minutes longer. Spoon peppers and sausages onto split and toasted bread for mammoth knife-and-fork sandwiches. Cut in large sections.

SAUSAGE IN ONION SAUCE

Double-smoked sausage and onions in beer sauce make a hot sandwich that you'll serve often in the summer. I had this first in a shady garden in New Jersey.

1 large roll smoked sausage, 2 to 2½ pounds
2 tablespoons butter
3 or 4 onions, peeled and sliced thin
1 (12-ounce) can beer
French roll–style sandwich buns, split, toasted
    and buttered

Makes

6 to 8

servings.

Place sausage on grill over hot coals. Grill, turning often, until browned, almost charred, 25 to 30 minutes. This extracts some of the fat from sausage. Meanwhile, in a 10- or 12-inch skillet at edge of grill melt butter. Pack onions tightly into melted butter. Add beer and heat to a boil. Simmer at edge of grill until onions are limp. Place sausage in sauce and turn until brown skin has colored sauce golden. Simmer 10 minutes.

Put sausage on board and slice. Layer onto bottom halves of buns and spoon onions over sausage, much as you would sauerkraut. Put tops on buns and serve on plates. This is a knife-and-fork sandwich.

BEEF AND VEAL

A thick steak, grilled juicy and rare inside and richly browned on the outside, is the American ideal of fine eating. This country's cattlemen and women produce the finest beef in the world, and there's no better way to cook tender beef than over a wood or charcoal fire. A men's club in Santa Maria, California, a farming community north of Santa Barbara, is famed for steak barbecue. Meat chefs grill 2½-inch-thick strip steaks over local red oak that burns so hot you wonder how the men can stand it. The racks of steaks are attached to pulley chains to assist in turning them. Now and then the Santa Maria club takes the barbecue show on the road, towing the equipment in trailers. They've cooked at Disneyland in Anaheim for the Democratic National Committee and at Republican wingdings, and most presidents in the last half century have had Santa Maria barbecue at least once. With the meat go pink beans grown near the town, salsa, potato salad, and garlic bread. Perhaps the most unusual outdoor steaks I've had were done in a farmyard near Bismarck, North Dakota. I was invited to judge the annual National Beef Cook-Off. The evening after cook day, contestants, judges, and other guests were asked to a "pitchfork barbecue." A ranch hand speared two or three steaks on a shiny-clean pitchfork and plunged the meat into a huge pot of bubbling hot suet for five or six minutes to cook it crusty and medium-rare. The steaks were pushed off the pitchforks onto platters and served with baked potatoes, coleslaw, and good bread.

A recipe isn't necessary for pitchfork barbecue. Use an iron pot—a large three-legged one about knee-high to sit over a fire on the ground—fill the pot about two-thirds full of suet. Build a fire big enough to keep the pot hot and melt the suet. Spear steaks on clean new pitchforks and lower them into the hot suet. And, of course, you need a stack of top-quality T-bone or porterhouse steaks.

Veal once was thought to be a no-no for barbecuing. That was before the pleasure of a grill-thick veal chop with herbs was discovered. I don't want a catsupy or peppery sauce on veal, but smoke does wonders for the mild flavor. Veal kebabs with peppers are a fine quick supper.

The recipes in this chapter represent a wide range of cookery styles, from true-blue American steaks and burgers to thin bits of meat seasoned Oriental style.

GRILLED STEAKS

A juicy thick steak grilled over charcoal is a rare treat, so once or twice a year I throw caution to the wind and grill a thick top-quality steak. For super steaks, find a good butcher. Buy prime or top-choice grade steaks 1½ to 2 inches thick. Fine marbling indicates tender meat. Coarse marbling usually indicates tough connective tissue. Club steaks are considered one-portion cuts. Sirloins, T-bones, porterhouse, or strip steaks are sliced for serving two or three people.

Remove steak from refrigerator 30 minutes to 1 hour before cooking. Most beef is trimmed lean. If not, trim the outer rim of fat to ⅛ inch.

Lay fire, using a single layer of charcoal a bit larger than the steak. Light it 45 minutes before starting to cook. Raise grill, if possible, to 5 inches for 2-inch-thick steak. Rub steak with olive oil or spray grill with nonstick spray. Place steak over fire. Grill until juices start to bubble on top of steak. Turn with tongs (a fork pierces meat and lets juice escape) until juice bubbles to top of second side. Continue cooking and turning until steak is done as desired.

A steak 2 inches thick cooks rare in a total of 15 to 18 minutes, medium in 20 to 22 minutes, and well-done in 25 to 27 minutes. Push instant-reading thermometer into the middle of steak, making sure tip does not go through or touch bone. Or slit steak with knife to check doneness.

Steaks 1½ inches thick require about 5 minutes less cooking time, and thicker steaks, up to 2½ inches, take about 20 minutes total time for rare, 25 for medium, and 30 for well-done. On a windy or cold day, cover grill or tent steak with aluminum foil to hold in heat, but leave the cover off in summer weather.

To serve, lift steak to a platter that has been warmed at the edge of the grill. Drizzle steak with olive oil or top with a pat of butter, let rest 3 or 4 minutes, and carve across the grain.

SALT, BEFORE OR AFTER

Do you salt before or after cooking? For barbecuing, some meat is rubbed with a seasoning mixture that contains salt before it is cooked. Other chefs preach no salt before food is cooked. Salt slows browning, they say.

The general rule of careful cooks is not to salt meats before grilling them. Dry beans should not be salted in the first stages of cooking, or they remain hard. Recipes here salt the beans about halfway through cooking.

But when I want special seasoning in meat, I bravely use a seasoning mix and most of them contain salt. Marinades with salt or soy sauce also are worth the slight chance that meat won't brown completely.

Vegetables and some kettle foods cooked in ample liquid can be salted early in the process.

Part of the drama of a beautiful steak is to sprinkle it with coarse salt and mill pepper onto it just before it comes off the grill. If you can stand the calories, a pat of butter goes on it, too.

HERBED TRIANGLE TIPS WITH VEGETABLES

This triangular piece of bottom sirloin has big flavor and can be tender if marinated and carved across the grain before serving. The vegetable kebabs are sumptuous-looking accompaniments to the meat.

1½ cups (2 medium) finely chopped onion

1 clove garlic, minced

2 tablespoons minced parsley

2 tablespoons fresh or 2 teaspoons dried thyme leaves

1 bay leaf, crumbled and spine discarded

¼ cup red wine vinegar

¼ cup olive oil

¼ cup water

2 triangle tips (bottom sirloins), 2 pounds each

Salt

8 mushrooms

1 large green bell pepper, cut in 8 strips

8 cherry tomatoes, stems removed

Makes 4 servings.

Combine onion, garlic, parsley, thyme, bay leaf, vinegar, oil, and water in a plastic food bag or deep bowl. Score curved surface of meat in diamond shapes and place in marinade. Turn to coat well and marinate 6 to 8 hours or overnight in refrigerator.

Build fire 45 minutes before cooking. Let burn down to hot coals. Remove meat from marinade and brush off onion bits. Coat grill with olive oil or vegetable cooking spray to prevent sticking. Place meat over fire. Pour marinade into small pan and warm at edge of grill. Turn and baste meat every 5 to 10 minutes. Grill 30 to 35 minutes, until juices in center run pink for medium-rare. Place on platter and tent with foil while cooking vegetables.

While meat is cooking prepare vegetables. Blanching prevents vegetables from splitting while threading on skewers. Bring large saucepan of water to a boil. Salt lightly and add mushrooms. Skim out after 30 seconds and cool quickly under cold running water. Add pepper strips to boiling water, remove after 1 minute, and cool promptly under cold running water. Alternate vegetables on 2 or 4 skewers, brush with marinade, and grill for 10 minutes, turning to brown evenly.

Cut meat in thin crosswise slices and arrange on plates with vegetables.

BEEF AND VEAL

JUICY THICK STEAK FOR TWO

Thick cuts of sirloin strip grilled over white-hot red oak are traditional for California's famed Santa Maria barbecue.

Merle Ellis, a butcher and syndicated columnist from Marin County, California, takes steak and trimmings East occasionally and once staged a Santa Maria–style barbecue on the shore in New Jersey for twenty-five guests. His choice of steak is triangle tip, a three-cornered piece of bottom sirloin cut when a sirloin is boned.

The well-marbled meat is juicy, tender, and full-flavored, says Ellis. It is less costly than the 2½-inch sirloin steaks customary in Santa Maria. The smaller tip steak bows to the rage for light eating without being skimpy.

Ask a meatman to order triangle tip for you, suggests Ellis, if he doesn't stock it. Suppliers ship them to markets, four bags to the box. If you buy a bag of tips (six to eight steaks, 1¾ to 2 pounds each), wrap and freeze tips individually, and thaw and cook as needed.

To grill triangle tip, marinate it or brush it with olive oil or butter and rub it with herbs. Grill it until it is done as you like. The bulging center section and tapered corners make very rare to medium-rare meat in the center and well-done meat at the corners possible. For rare meat at the center, grill 15 to 20 minutes, turning once or twice. Slice the tip to serve. Each steak provides generous servings for two, or even three.

The triangle tip is a favorite roasting cut with couples. It offers the rich flavor of a beef roast, but without the overwhelming leftovers and cost of the large roast. A tip can be roasted on a rack in an open pan at 325 degrees for about an hour and a quarter or at 425 degrees for 45 to 50 minutes.

TEXAS BARBECUED BRISKET

Long, slow cooking on indirect heat produces the barbecue that Texans love best. A kettle-cooked version of this is given on page 212. Mesquite chips give true Texas flavor, but use hickory chips if mesquite is not available.

1 piece beef brisket, 3½ pounds

1 cup catsup

½ cup cider vinegar

¼ cup Worcestershire sauce

½ stick (¼ cup) butter

3 ribs celery, finely chopped

1 onion, finely chopped

2 cloves garlic, minced

1 fresh or canned green chile, seeded and minced, or

     2 teaspoons chili powder

1 teaspoon paprika

½ teaspoon salt

½ teaspoon freshly ground pepper

Makes 6 to 8 servings.

Put 2 or 3 handfuls of mesquite or hickory chips in bucket of water to soak 4 or 5 hours. Build fire 45 minutes to 1 hour before cooking. Build another fire in auxiliary grill to supply hot coals to add as needed. When fire has burned down to hot coals, spread to provide moderate heat, and fit drip pan in front or in center of coals.

Trim fat from meat, leaving a ⅛-inch layer. Place brisket on grill over drip pan. Cover grill and adjust dampers to maintain slow, steady heat.

As beef starts to cook, combine all other ingredients in saucepan. Simmer 10 minutes and remove from heat. After 1 hour, baste brisket lightly with sauce. Turn meat occasionally to cook evenly and baste lightly. Replenish fire with hot coals, but do not pile coals. Brisket should cook slowly 4 to 5 hours, until meat almost falls apart.

Sprinkle chips over coals. Cover grill with vents closed and let meat smoke 15 to 20 minutes. Remove cover and brush meat with sauce. Place meat on board and slice. It will crumble. Serve meat and remaining sauce on buttered sandwich buns.

Leftover sandwiches can be frozen and reheated in a microwave or conventional oven, or the shredded meat and sauce can be frozen together to reheat for sandwiches.

REAL TEXAS BARBECUE

"If you have ever ordered barbecue in such outrageous places as New York or Los Angeles, you will understand from experience the murderous rage that lives in us all. You may even break down and cry in a public place. There is nothing like Texas barbecue. It is one of those things that simply doesn't export. . . . Grilling over charcoal will produce a marvelous steak or lamb chop or even chicken, but that is not barbecue. Barbecue is smoke, and not too much heat, and plenty of time. You can barbecue less-than-choice cuts. You cannot grill them. It takes low heat to tenderize a brisket. . . . Wes Gulley does a good job of home barbecuing, using his modified oil-drum barbecue pit. He builds a parsimonious little fire at one end of the drum, puts the meat at the other end, closes the lid, and barbecues away. Wes seasons the meat dry, then mops the meat with a sauce about every half hour; he cooks his barbecue at least 4 hours no matter what meat. When he mops the meat, he dabs it on, since dragging the mop across the meat would knock off the dry seasonings." — *The Only Texas Cookbook* by Linda West Eckhardt, Texas Monthly Press, 1981.

MATAMORAS AGUJAS
(BEEF CHUCK RIBS)

This meaty cut with four or five "feather ribs" in it can be cooked without a sauce, but this method complements the meaty flavor.

¼ cup vegetable oil

2 tablespoons wine vinegar

2 cloves garlic, minced

2 *agujas*, ¾ inch thick and 1¼ pounds each

1 teaspoon ground cumin

Salt and freshly ground pepper to taste

Makes 2 large servings.

Combine oil, vinegar, and garlic. Mix well. Oil grill rack or spritz with nonstick spray. Rub cumin on meat, then place meat on grill over hot coals. Brush lightly with oil mixture. Grill 5 to 7 minutes, turn, brush again with sauce, and grill until rare to medium-rare, 5 minutes longer. Season to taste and serve with hot tortillas, salsa, and Frijoles Refritos. Meat is cut from bones to eat.

MATAMOROS AGUJAS

Agujas (pronounced ah-GOO-hahs) has been barbecued over mesquite in Matamoros, Mexico, for a century or more. A few years ago, it moved north of the Rio Grande, and demand is so heavy that H&H Foods of Mercedes, Texas, a major supplier, no longer has enough to fill orders from venturesome chefs and home cooks in other areas.

A meat cutter who rises to a challenge and has access to whole carcasses or sides of beef can cut agujas for you. There are two cuts of agujas to a carcass. Each is the first four to six feather bones of the forequarter. It is a flat piece of meat, about ¾ inch thick, with meat surrounding the bones. The meat is eaten off the bone by some aficionados or is cut and served off the bones.

Agujas is called beef chuck ribs by some, but technically is a portion of chuck. The name means "needle," referring to the pointed ends of the bones.

Meat merchandisers in Texas tout the glories of agujas— lots of lean meat, simple preparation, and good meaty flavor.

HERBED BEEF FILLET

1 beef fillet, about 5 pounds

1 stick (1/2 cup) butter

1 tablespoon minced fresh or 1 teaspoon dried tarragon

1 tablespoon minced fresh or 1 teaspoon dried chervil

1 tablespoon minced shallots or scallions

2 tablespoons dry white wine

2 tablespoons white wine vinegar

Makes 8 to 10 servings.

Buy a prime fillet, if possible, and fold under and tie tail to form a roast of uniform thickness. Melt butter in a small saucepan. Stir in tarragon, chervil, and shallots or scallions. Cook over very low heat a minute or 2. Slowly stir in wine and vinegar and heat slowly. Place meat on a tray and brush with herbed butter. Let stand at room temperature 1 hour, brushing with sauce 2 or 3 times. Remove meat from tray and pour any sauce remaining on tray into saucepan with remaining sauce.

Brown fillet over coals on all sides for about 10 minutes, watching carefully to prevent fire flare-ups. Move meat to edge of grill or cover grill and adjust dampers to maintain slow steady heat. Grill 15 to 20 minutes longer or until fillet is done as desired. Heat remaining sauce at edge of grill and serve with sliced fillet.

GRILLED FILLET WITH MUSHROOM SAUCE

This lightly hickory-smoked fillet is a favorite of my dear friend Jim Beard. He likes it very rare. The sliced fillet makes good luncheon sandwiches.

1 beef fillet, about 4½ pounds

½ cup red wine

¼ cup oil

¼ cup minced onion

1 tablespoon herbes de Provence or other herb blend

Mushroom Sauce (recipe follows)

Makes 6 to 8 servings.

Buy prime-grade fillet, if possible, and trim it well. Fold and tie the tail to the meat to form a roast of uniform thickness (or have butcher do it for you). Place meat in a plastic bag. Mix wine, oil, onion, and herbs. Pour over the meat, close bag tightly, and turn it to coat meat with marinade. Place bag in a dish and marinate meat 2 hours at room temperature or overnight in refrigerator. Drain meat, reserving marinade.

Grill meat 4 inches above hot coals, turning to brown all sides. This takes about 10 minutes of undivided attention so you can put out any flash fires. Add damp hickory chips or small hickory sticks. Move meat to edge of grill or cover grill and cook 15 to 20 minutes longer for rare, 20 to 25 minutes for medium-rare. Slice and serve with Mushroom Sauce.

MUSHROOM SAUCE

2 tablespoons butter

2 tablespoons minced onion

2 cloves garlic, minced

8 ounces fresh mushrooms, cleaned and sliced

1 teaspoon meat glaze (Bovril) or broth seasoning mix

Reserved marinade for fillet

Red wine or beef broth, if needed

Makes 6 to 8 servings.

In a medium skillet melt butter, add onion and garlic, and cook until onion is tender but not browned. Add mushrooms and cook, stirring gently now and then, until well saturated with butter and most of the juices cooked from mushrooms have evaporated. Stir in meat glaze. Add reserved marinade and, if needed, a few tablespoons wine or broth to make a light sauce. Serve hot with grilled fillet.

BARBECUED BEEF RIBS

"Ribs for barbecue" were abundant in markets for a few years, now I find them only occasionally. Though they are scarce, it is worth knowing this special cut. The ribs grill crusty and have a big bone to gnaw on after you've cut off the dainty slivers of meat. Make sure you get rib bones; short ribs are too tough to barbecue.*

> 2 or 3 rib bones per person
> Barbecue Sauce of your choice (pages 190–203) or
>   Dijon-style mustard

Place ribs rounded side down on grill 3 to 4 inches above hot coals. Brown, turn, and brown the other side. Brush lightly with barbecue sauce or mustard. Cook and turn until done as desired, about 10 minutes for ribs with an average amount of sauce. Heat sauce at edge of grill and serve at table with ribs, or pass extra mustard.

GRILLED SKIRT STEAK

This flat fibrous steak is richly flavored when grilled over charcoal, and the marinade enhances the effect. Don't overcook a skirt steak or it will be dry and tough.*

> 1 teaspoon dry mustard
> 1 teaspoon ground cumin
> 1 bay leaf, crumbled
> 1 clove garlic, minced
> 1 cup well-seasoned beef broth, heated to boiling
> ¼ cup Worcestershire sauce
> 1 tablespoon cider vinegar
> 1 tablespoon oil
> 1 teaspoon hot pepper sauce
> 2 skirt steaks, about 12 ounces each

Makes 4 servings.

In a small bowl or 2-cup measure blend mustard, cumin, bay leaf, and garlic. Add boiling broth and mix well, mashing any lumps of mustard against side of bowl or cup. Stir in Worcestershire sauce, vinegar, oil, and pepper sauce. Cover and let cool.

Place steaks in a plastic bag or shallow dish, add marinade, turn, and let marinate 2 to 3 hours at room temperature, turning 2 or 3 times. Remove meat from marinade and grill 4 to 5 inches above hot coals until well browned, 6 to 8 minutes; turn and brown other side for 6 to 8 minutes. Brush with marinade and serve at once.

Any leftover marinade can be frozen and reused.

LEMON–GARLIC FLANK STEAK

Many regard this as the tastiest of all steaks. But be sure to carve it immediately after it comes off the grill—otherwise, the fibers tighten and the steak becomes leathery. Have a sharp knife and board ready to slice it thin across the grain. Any extras should be sliced immediately and kept in the refrigerator for tomorrow's lunch.

1 flank steak, about 1½ pounds

½ medium sweet onion, thinly sliced and separated
    into rings

⅓ cup lemon juice

1 clove garlic, split

1 tablespoon sugar

½ teaspoon salt

2 tablespoons soy sauce

Makes 4 to 6 servings.

Pull off any membrane from steak and trim away any surface fat. Score steak ⅛ inch deep on both sides in diamond pattern. In plastic bag or glass dish large enough to hold steak, combine onion, lemon juice, garlic, sugar, salt, and soy sauce. Add steak, close bag tightly if using, and turn meat to coat thoroughly. Marinate 1 to 2 hours at room temperature, 6 to 8 hours in the refrigerator. Drain off and reserve marinade.

Grill steak 3 to 5 inches above hot coals until rare to medium-rare, 3 to 5 minutes on each side. Meanwhile, heat remaining marinade. Remove steak to a cutting board and cut in thin slices across the grain, slanting knife slightly. Serve meat with hot marinade.

BEEF–FILLED ONIONS

3 large onions
1½ pounds lean ground beef
1 egg, slightly beaten
1 teaspoon salt
Florida or Texas Barbecue Sauce (page 192 or 194)

Makes 6 servings.

Cut onions in half crosswise, pull off skins, and scoop out centers, leaving sturdy shells. Chop scooped-out onion. Combine beef, egg, salt, ¾ cup sauce, and the chopped onion. Mix well and shape into 6 large meatballs. Cut 6 squares of heavy-duty foil large enough to contain each onion half, and place an onion half on each of the squares. Put a meatball in each onion half and spoon a little sauce over the combination. Fold foil up around onions and seal tightly, allowing space in foil packets for steam.

Grill 4 to 6 inches above hot coals about 30 minutes. Protecting hands with mitts, peel back foil so tops of meat and onions are exposed. Baste with drippings in foil packets or with additional sauce. Cover grill or shape a loose tent of foil over onions and continue cooking 25 minutes longer or until onions are as tender as desired and meat is done to taste.

GRILLED CALF'S LIVER STEAK

My *friend Jerome Schilling, an architect, literally designed his home in Miami Shores, Florida, around the barbecue grill. You open the front door and are greeted with a dramatic vista of a tropical garden, then move through the living room, past his wife Louise's artfully set table, to the kitchen. The kitchen opens onto the grill, built to the leeward side to prevent cooking fumes from wafting indoors. There Jerome cooks. He has introduced me to dozens of the delights of barbecuing, and I particularly enjoy feasting on this thick liver steak when I visit the Schillings.*

2 pounds calf's liver, cut 1 to 1½ inches thick

1 large onion, cut in 4 slices

1 stick (½ cup) butter, melted

Salt and freshly ground pepper

Juice of ½ lemon

4 slices bacon, cooked crisp

Makes 4 generous servings.

Dip liver and onion slices in melted butter and place on grill 4 to 6 inches above hot fire. Grill until liver and onion are browned; turn and grill the other sides. Place onion on top of liver and grill until meat is done as desired. The liver is best if crusty on the outside and still pink inside. Cut a slit in the center of each piece of liver to test for doneness.

Remove liver to a small platter and cut in thin slices. Season with salt, pepper, and lemon juice. Arrange onion slices and bacon on platter around liver.

BEEF AND VEAL

FAJITAS

Fajitas make a convivial summertime party. Grill the meat, recruit helpers for carving it, and let guests layer on trimmings from a buffet table.

2 pounds skirt steak or 1½ pounds top round,
    1 inch thick
Juice of 1 lemon
2 tablespoons vegetable oil
½ teaspoon coarsely ground pepper
Salt, optional
8 flour tortillas
2 cups Frijoles Refritos (page 218)
½ bunch green onions or scallions, sliced thin
½ bunch cilantro, leaves only
1 small avocado, sliced and dipped in lemon juice
½ pint sour cream
Pico de Gallo (page 199)

Makes 4 servings.

Trim surface fat and stringy membrane from meat. Pierce round steak with fork to allow marinade to penetrate. Stir together lemon juice and oil. Place meat in plastic food bag or shallow dish and marinate in lemon-oil mixture for 15 to 20 minutes. Remove meat from marinade, reserving lemon-oil. Pat meat dry and coat heavily with pepper.

Place meat over hot coals, brush lightly with lemon-oil, and grill 12 to 15 minutes, until meat juices show pink when slit with knife near center. Remove to board, cover with foil, and let rest 5 minutes. Salt meat to taste and cut across the grain in very thin slices.

For each fajita, your guest fills a hot tortilla with a few slices of beef, spoonful of beans, sprinkle of green onion or scallion and cilantro, avocado slice, spoonful of sour cream, and sauce to taste. Fold tortilla in half and enjoy.

FROM RANCH TO TRENDY RESTAURANTS

Fajitas began as simple ranch fare in Texas, a way to use skirt steaks, also called the hanging tender or butcher's steak, deliciously. The meat is tender and best when fresh, so fajitas were grilled by chuck wagon cooks the evening of a slaughter.

Fajitas combine foods that most Texans adore, so it was only natural that home barbecue chefs adopted this savory beef dish. Fajitas parties have become regular weekend entertainment in Western Texas and are moving East to Dallas and Houston. The host or hostess grills the meat and guests plunk a steak strip into a tortilla and fill in the trimmings.

Then fajitas moved to trendy restaurants in New York, Los Angeles, San Francisco, Kansas City, and Chicago. Fast food places have them, not the same as a Texas range hand's fare, but beef and trimmings of a sort.

Trendiness tends to corrupt folk food, so chefs serve chicken cutlet, tuna, and we even heard of alligator fajitas in Florida.

They're fun anyway you fill them, but beef is the original. If you can't get skirt steak, a hunk of top round is good, and flank steak makes delicious fajitas.

FAJITAS BY ANY NAME

Fajitas means "little girdles," and logically for the authentic cut of meat. The skirt steak is a tender but fibrous strip of meat cut from inside the diaphragm section of a carcass, where the animal would wear a girdle if beef animals indulged in such wear.

If you shop for a girdle in a Mexican women's lingerie shop, you ask for a *faja*. Hence the descriptive name given this cut of beef grilled, cut in strips, and rolled in a tortilla with sauce and trimmings.

A terrible shortage of skirt steaks is created by the popularity of fajitas. There are only two skirt steaks, each weighing 1½ to 2 pounds, in each carcass. Now fajitas are made of top round, chuck, flank, and other less tender cuts of beef when skirt steak is unobtainable. And skirt steaks go for about the price of sirloin strip in some parts of country. Formerly they were priced at about half the cost of top-grade tender steaks and until recently were used primarily for stews, except by those few who recognized the skirt steak as a tender steak when grilled quickly and rare.

ROAST BEEF IN BOURBON SAUCE

This beef is roasted on a spit, or you can do it on a flat grill if you keep the fire moderate and use a drip pan.

1/2 cup oil

1/2 cup bourbon

1 onion, thinly sliced

2 cloves garlic, minced

1 teaspoon freshly ground pepper

1 teaspoon dry mustard

1 teaspoon salt

1/4 cup wine or cider vinegar

1 rib-eye or tied prime or choice grade first-cut chuck
     or boneless beef round, 5 to 6 pounds

Makes 10 to 12 generous servings.

Combine oil, bourbon, onion, garlic, pepper, mustard, salt, and vinegar. Place meat in plastic bag or dish. Pour marinade over meat and marinate 1 hour at room temperature, turning meat 2 or 3 times.

Drain meat, reserving marinade. Spit meat from end to end through center or on a diagonal, making sure roast is balanced. If the meat has not already been tied, tie it after you have fastened it in place with spit forks—it will be a little firmer that way.

Engage spit and turn meat 8 to 10 inches above hot coals 1½ hours (or until meat thermometer registers 120 degrees) for rare, to 2½ hours for well-done (165 degrees internal temperature). Brush with sauce last 30 minutes of cooking. To roast on grill, place meat over drip pan with hot coals surrounding it or pushed to back, and turn and baste meat as needed to cook evenly. Grill 1½ to 2½ hours. Let meat stand on platter 20 to 30 minutes before carving. Heat sauce and serve with meat.

Leftovers make grand sandwiches and beef salad.

PEPPERED ROUND STEAK

1/3 cup olive oil

1 1/2 to 2 pounds top round steak, 1 1/2 inches thick

2 tablespoons balsamic or red wine vinegar

Freshly ground pepper

Makes 4
generous
servings.

Heat oil until very warm, not sizzling. Place meat in a shallow dish and pierce all over with a fork. Turn and pierce other side. Pour half the warm oil on meat and poke with fork so oil penetrates meat fibers. Turn and repeat process on the other side. Pour vinegar over steak and turn. Cover and marinate at room temperature about 2 hours or in refrigerator overnight, turning and piercing meat occasionally. Remove meat, reserving marinade, and sprinkle pepper over generously, pressing it in with the heel of the hand.

Grill meat 3 inches above hot coals until browned; turn and grill other side. Move to edge of grill and continue cooking until done as desired. This steak is most tender if grilled rare, about 18 minutes' total cooking time, or medium-rare, about 22 minutes. Place on warm platter and slice across the grain. Serve with Shallot Cream (recipe follows), if desired.

SHALLOT CREAM

2 tablespoons marinade for Peppered Round Steak

1 tablespoon minced shallots

1 cup heavy cream

Salt and coarsely ground pepper

In a small skillet heat marinade. Stir in shallots and cook until lightly browned. Stir in cream and cook, stirring often, until slightly reduced. Season to taste with salt and pepper. Serve with steak.

BISTECES RANCHEROS

Near my New York apartment, a pretty little restaurant with a few Taos-style paintings hanging on the pink walls serves this spicy supper dish. If you can get good tortillas, this is a snap to make—a good beefy flavor with Tex-Mex verve.

2 pounds chuck steak

1 clove garlic, smashed

1/3 cup olive oil

12 corn tortillas

2 or 3 canned long green chiles, cut in 12 strips

Santa Maria Salsa (page 250)

Makes 6 servings.

Cut steak into fingers 1 by 1 by 3 inches. In a plastic bag combine steak with garlic and oil. Close tightly and turn to coat meat well. Marinate at room temperature for 1 to 1½ hours.

Grill steak 3 to 4 inches from hot coals, turning to brown evenly. Meat should be rare to medium-rare. This takes 10 to 12 minutes' total cooking time.

Meanwhile, wrap tortillas in a clean kitchen towel and heat in a 325-degree oven. As meat comes off fire, place a strip of steak and a strip of chile in each tortilla and roll up. Serve with Santa Maria Salsa. Two of these fat tortilla sandwiches make a nice portion, served with refried beans or beans and rice.

BEEF SATAY

The first time I ate grilled skewered beef strongly seasoned with lime juice, honey, soy sauce, and spices was in a restaurant operated by an Indonesian man in Santa Monica, California. Since then I've had similar skewered beef or pork in the Thai restaurants that are springing up all over the country, as well as in Indian, Malaysian, and Vietnamese restaurants.

2 pounds beef sirloin or fillet

½ cup soy sauce

2 tablespoons honey

2 tablespoons lime juice

1 tablespoon curry powder

1 teaspoon chili powder

1 medium onion, minced

2 cloves garlic, minced

Makes 6 main-dish servings; 12 to 15 appetizer servings.

Cut meat in 1-inch cubes and place in a bowl or plastic bag. In a 2-cup measure combine soy sauce, honey, lime juice, curry and chili powders, onion, and garlic. Mix thoroughly and pour over meat. Marinate 30 minutes at room temperature. Thread meat on bamboo skewers that have been soaked in water to prevent charring or on small metal skewers. Push meat close together if some rare portions are wanted, space it slightly for well-done meat.

Grill 2 to 3 inches above hot coals until done as desired, about 8 minutes total for medium-rare.

ORIENTAL SHORT–RIB BARBECUE

This recipe with the toasty taste of sesame oil and seeds and zest of red pepper and ginger took first prize in the National Beef Cook-Off in 1988 when I was chairman of barbecue judges. In the East, the rib section used here is called flanken.

¾ cup thinly sliced green onion or scallions

½ cup soy sauce

½ cup water

¼ cup Oriental-style dark sesame oil

2½ tablespoons firmly packed brown sugar

1½ tablespoons toasted sesame seeds, crushed (see Note)

1 tablespoon minced garlic

1 tablespoon grated ginger root

½ teaspoon ground red pepper

⅛ teaspoon crushed red pepper pods

4 pounds well-trimmed beef rib short ribs

Makes 12 servings.

Combine green onions, soy sauce, water, sesame oil, brown sugar, sesame seeds, garlic, ginger, red pepper, and crushed red pepper. Place meat in a plastic food bag and add marinade, turning to coat well. Marinate in refrigerator 4 to 6 hours, turning bag now and then. Remove ribs and reserve marinade.

Oil grill or spritz with nonstick cooking spray. Place meat on grill 5 to 6 inches above hot coals. Grill until done as wished, about 12 minutes, turning once and brushing with marinade before turning.

Note: To toast sesame seeds, spread in dry heavy skillet and stir over moderate heat until light tan color. Take care not to scorch.

FLANKEN

Flanken-cut ribs are a thin cut of rib ends, not short ribs, so they are a relatively tender section. Ask your butcher to order them for you, if he does not regularly stock them.

The trade name for this cut is rib section short ribs. To get this cut, ask the meat dealer to make ½-inch cuts across the sixth, seventh, and eighth ribs. Each rib steak will contain three cross rib bones and a good-eating slab of beef.

Flanken is a Yiddish word for flank steak, but it has been used as a name for rib section short ribs for many years.

KIELBASA GRILL ALFRESCO

A *fast-cooking skewerful of spicy sausage, apple, and onion is a good thought for a campfire breakfast, or a nourishing supper when you are too tired or rushed to fuss.*

1 pound kielbasa or Polish sausage

2 or 3 firm, tart apples (McIntosh, Ida Red, Jonathan, or Granny Smith)

2 or 3 onions

Makes 4 to 6 servings.

Cut kielbasa in 1½-inch slices. Wash and cut unpeeled apples in 4 to 6 wedges each. Peel onions and cut in half, then in wedges. You will need 8 to 12 wedges. Thread sausage chunks with apple and onion wedges on skewers, alternating meat with apple and onion and starting and ending with sausage. Apples and onions should be speared diagonally so they don't slip off while cooking.

Grill 3 inches above hot coals until browned and done as desired, about 12 minutes' total cooking for juicy but well-cooked sausage. Push meat and accompaniments off skewers onto warm plates, using a fork. Serve with mustard along with baked potatoes or poppyseed noodles.

BEEF TERIYAKI

Tangy sweet teriyaki sauce perks up steaks or hamburgers, but accordion-threaded skewers of thin-cut beef make the traditional Japanese teriyaki.

1 top round or chuck steak, at least 1 inch thick,
    2 to 3 pounds
½ cup catsup
¼ cup teriyaki sauce
¼ cup water
2 tablespoons honey
1 clove garlic, minced

Makes 4 to 6 main-dish servings.

Partially freeze meat, then with very sharp knife cut into almost paper-thin strips across the grain. There should be 3 to 4 strips of meat for each person. Fold meat accordion-style onto bamboo skewers that have been soaked in water to prevent charring or short metal skewers. Place in a shallow bowl or plastic bag. Combine catsup, teriyaki sauce, water, honey, and garlic. Mix well and pour over meat on skewers. Turn and marinate in sauce about 30 minutes.

Grill 2 to 3 inches over hot fire on hibachi or small grill until browned, but not dried out, about 4 minutes' total cooking time. Serve as hors d'oeuvres or as a main dish with rice and Japanese-style vegetables.

BEEF AND VEAL

KOREAN BEEF BARBECUE

This fast barbecue holds to the Oriental system of thin-cut meat to conserve precious fuel. Use a hibachi or small grill, since a big fire will still be burning long after the meat is cooked.

1½ pounds boneless beef chuck, round, or sirloin, cut 1 inch thick

1 tablespoon sesame seeds

1 cup finely chopped scallions (2 large)

2 to 3 cloves garlic, minced

¼ cup soy sauce

2 tablespoons sugar

2 tablespoons dry sherry

2 tablespoons vegetable oil

Makes 4 to 6 servings.

Freeze meat until firm, about 2 hours. Meanwhile, in a heavy skillet spread sesame seeds and toast over moderate heat until golden. Stir seeds once or twice to toast evenly. With mortar and pestle or with back of a spoon against a board, grind seeds until powdery. Place in a large bowl with scallions, garlic, soy sauce, sugar, sherry, and oil. Mix well.

With a very sharp knife, cut semifrozen meat across the grain into strips about ¼ inch thick. Add meat strips to sauce, stir to coat meat well, cover, and marinate at room temperature 1 to 2 hours.

Let fire in hibachi or small grill burn down to glowing coals. If grill rack is widely spaced, place meat strips in a hinged wire broiler. Broil about 1 minute on each side until browned but still rare. Serve with rice and vinegary coleslaw or cucumber salad.

STUFFED HAMBURGERS PLUS

Plump burgers grilled over wood or charcoal fire are plenty good, but a filling makes them a Saturday night special for guests. The fillings can also be used as toppings, if you prefer.

2 pounds lean ground beef (see Note)

4 to 6 ounces sharp Cheddar cheese

Barbecue sauce of your choice (pages 190–203)

Makes 6 thick stuffed patties.

Shape the meat into 12 thin patties, pressing just enough to make meat cling together. Cut cheese in slivers and arrange on half the patties, leaving space to seal edges. Place remaining patties over cheese and press edges firmly to seal.

Grill 4 to 5 inches above hot coals until browned on both sides, turning as needed to cook evenly. Cook until done as desired, about 10 minutes' total cooking for rare, 12 to 15 minutes for medium, and 15 to 18 minutes for well-done. Serve hot on toasted buns with catsup, mustard, pickle relish, or other condiments.

Note: Beef labeled lean or ground chuck, not very lean or leanest, makes juicy burgers without excessive shrinking.

OTHER FILLINGS:

Cheese spread: pepper-flavored, herb-flavored, or chive cheese—a good way to use up leftover party cheeses.

Butter blended half and half with crumbled Roquefort or other blue cheese; a flavored butter (see pages 204–06); 6 tablespoons soft butter blended with 1 to 2 tablespoons Dijon-style mustard or prepared horseradish.

Mushrooms and shallots sautéed in butter; thinly sliced tomato or green pepper rings; sliced onion.

HOLLYWOOD BURGERS

Back in the sixties, one of the first stylish "health food" restaurants in Hollywood, the Aware Inn, served plump juicy hamburgers like these.

1½ pounds ground lean beef

1½ cups shredded Cheddar cheese

½ cup each chopped seeded fresh tomato, seeded green
     pepper, and onion

½ teaspoon sea salt or kosher salt

Freshly ground pepper to taste

Makes 4 large or 6 medium-size servings.

Combine beef, cheese, tomato, green pepper, onion, salt, and pepper to taste. Work together with hands until well mixed. Shape into patties, pressing gently to make meat and vegetables cling together.

Grease grill well. Place patties on grill 3 to 4 inches above hot coals and grill until well browned, turning to cook evenly. Cook until done as desired, rare in about 12 minutes, medium in about 15, and well-done in 18 to 20 minutes.

HAMBURGERS WITH CHILI

2 cups chili con carne, leftover homemade or canned

1½ cups shredded Cheddar cheese

½ cup California red table wine

1½ pounds lean ground beef

½ teaspoon salt

2 tablespoons grated onion

4 slices toasted French bread

Makes 4 generous servings.

In a small saucepan combine chili, cheese, and wine. Heat at edge of grill, stirring now and then, until cheese is melted and blended into chili. Meanwhile, mix beef, salt, and onion. Shape into 4 patties about 1 inch thick.

Grill 3 to 4 inches above hot coals until done as desired, 10 to 12 minutes for medium-rare. Place on toast and spoon cheese chili over them.

LONDON BROIL

*F*lank steak is the traditional cut for London broil, though a thick top round is labeled London Broil in some markets. The marinade works on either cut.

1 flank steak or top round, 1½ to 2 pounds

1 large clove garlic, split

2 tablespoons oil

1 tablespoon red wine vinegar

Salt and freshly ground pepper

1 stick (½ cup) butter

¼ cup beef broth

¼ cup dry red wine

1 teaspoon Worcestershire sauce

2 tablespoons minced fresh parsley

1 tablespoon minced scallion tops

Makes

4 to 6

servings.

Cut meat on each side into 1½-inch diamonds about ⅛ inch deep. Rub with garlic and place in a shallow dish. Sprinkle with oil, vinegar, and salt and pepper to taste. Turn in dish, cover, and marinate at room temperature 30 to 45 minutes.

Meanwhile, melt butter and stir in broth, wine, Worcestershire sauce, parsley, and scallions. Keep warm on edge of grill.

Grill steak 3 to 4 inches above hot coals 4 to 5 minutes on each side for flank, 6 to 8 minutes for round. Do not overcook, or flank steak will be tough. Immediately remove to board and, holding knife almost parallel with meat, carve in very thin diagonal slices. Serve with the wine and herb sauce.

AL VELA'S EL MOLINO VIEJO

The excuse for driving the horrendous road from Los Angeles to San Quintin Bay in Baja California—it was in the sixties and some of the road was unpaved, dusty, and full of ruts— was to fish. But the reason Jim and Ann Hanyen, my husband, and I chose Al Vela's El Molino Viejo over other more accessible places was his table. Al always cooked, with the help of local women and his wife, Dorothy. Having grown up in Sonora, Al worked in Santa Monica, California, for a few years, then took his young family to San Quintin to operate a sardine cannery. In the fifties, when sardine fisheries lagged, he converted the canning plant to a hunting and fishing lodge. His meals became legendary, drawing many a traveler.

I remember the night Al served barbecued local beef, always of dubious quality, with Mexican coarse corn, fresh snap beans, and a pie that Dorothy had made of canned condensed milk and limes, just plucked from the tree. The food at El Molino was particularly remarkable because Al had to depend on pantry items—it was 100 miles to Ensenada and the nearest grocery store.

I can also recall the reaction of a young Frenchwoman, a reluctant guest whose husband had lost his way on the dreadful road, when she tasted Al's beef, fresh corn dressed simply with cream, finely chopped onion, and fresh cilantro. Her eyes lit up and she said, "You've done something special to this food!" Al always stands near to hear comments and insure good service by the waitresses. At the Frenchwoman's comment, he brought out bottles of Cabernet Sauvignon, Baja-made by a gifted winegrower.

I had found Al barbecuing the beef the afternoon before. I recognized it as a Mexican-cut beef, in nondescript hunks. Al swore me to secrecy. The beef had been slaughtered a few miles away that morning. Al sped back to the lodge with it and refrigerated the meat to take the body heat out of it. I found him searing it rapidly over a charcoal fire, then braising it gently in a skillet of barbecue sauce. "You have to nurse this beef along," Al explained.

AL VELA'S BARBECUED BEEF

If you get beef that is not up to your expectations, or have a less tender cut, try Al's method.

2 pounds beef round, chuck, or shank, cut in serving-
  size pieces
Barbecue sauce of your choice (pages 190–203)

*Makes
6 to 8
servings.*

Brown meat quickly on grill 3 to 4 inches above very hot coals to seal in juices. At edge of grill heat about ½ inch of barbecue sauce in a large skillet with a cover. As each small steak is browned, place it in the sauce. After all the meat is seared and piled in the skillet, brush lightly with additional sauce, cover the skillet, and braise meat 10 minutes, just until moist and heated through, but not well-done. If overcooked, the meat will be dry and stringy. Spread hot coals out to lower heat. With tongs, lift steaks onto grill over moderate heat and cook just long enough to crisp the surface. Serve at once with any leftover sauce, if desired.

CHUCK STEAK WITH DEVILED SAUCE

1 chuck steak, 2½ pounds, about 1½ inches thick
Olive oil
¼ cup finely chopped scallions
½ cup soy sauce
¼ cup catsup
1 tablespoon prepared mustard
1 teaspoon freshly ground pepper

Makes 4 to 6 servings.

Place steak in dish and puncture with fork in several places, then drizzle with olive oil. In a small saucepan combine 2 tablespoons olive oil, the scallions, soy sauce, catsup, mustard, and pepper. Heat until well blended and just boiling.

Meanwhile, grill steak 2 to 3 inches above hot coals until browned on both sides, about 30 minutes for medium-rare. Place steak on platter and carve across the grain in ¼-inch slices. Serve 2 or 3 slices per person, with sauce on the side.

WARM BEEF AND GREENS SALAD

I took this to a potluck supper at church one spring evening. It was such a hit that I barely got a bite myself.

¾ pound beef top round, sliced across the grain
    in strips ½ inch thick
½ teaspoon minced ginger root
1 clove garlic, minced
1 teaspoon dry sherry
½ teaspoon soy sauce
½ teaspoon sugar
1½ teaspoons oyster sauce
½ teaspoon Oriental-style sesame oil
1 teaspoon cornstarch
Dash hot pepper sauce
1 pound spinach, escarole, or romaine, or mixture
½ small red onion, cut and separated into rings

Makes 4 servings.

Place meat in plastic food bag or deep bowl. In another bowl combine ginger, garlic, sherry, soy sauce, sugar, oyster sauce, oil, cornstarch, and pepper sauce. Mix and pour over meat, seal bag, or cover and marinate in refrigerator 2 hours or longer.

While meat is marinating, wash and dry greens, and shred. Place in salad bowl and distribute onion rings over top. Remove meat from marinade and pour marinade into saucepan. Brush grill with vegetable oil or spray with nonstick cooking spray. Or put meat in hinged grill for easier turning. Grill meat until browned, but not too well done. Add hot meat and warmed marinade to greens, toss and serve.

GRILLED VEAL CHOPS

Lightly seasoned veal chops grilled quickly over charcoal or a wood fire in a fireplace are juicy and full of flavor.

4 veal loin or shoulder chops, about ¾ inch thick
Salt and freshly ground pepper
Marjoram or thyme
Olive oil
Wine vinegar or lemon juice

Makes 4 servings.

Place veal on a platter and sprinkle lightly with seasonings of choice. Drizzle oil over veal, using about ½ teaspoonful for each side of each chop. Sprinkle with vinegar or lemon juice.

Place 3 to 4 inches over hot fire and grill until browned. Turn and brown other side. Total cooking time will be about 8 minutes. Do not overcook or veal will be tough.

Serve with sautéed mushrooms and boiled potatoes or Country-Fried Potatoes (see page 242).

VEAL AND HAM KEBABS

Prosciutto is a flavormaker for veal, as in Saltimbocca, an Italian-American dish of veal steaks filled with thinly-sliced prosciutto and cheese, then sautéed in butter and olive oil. Prosciutto is air-dried ham Italian style and is excellent, but tends to dry out on the grill. Any ham you have, plus sage and olive oil, enhances the mild veal flavor in this dish.

1½ pounds leg of veal, in 1-inch cubes
1 tablespoon minced fresh or ½ teaspoon dried
    rubbed sage
1 pound ham, cooked or cook-before-eating type,
    in 1-inch cubes
3 tablespoons olive oil
1 tablespoon dry marsala wine
2 medium red bell peppers, cut in squares
Salt and freshly ground pepper

Makes 4 servings.

Place veal, sage, ham, oil, and wine in shallow bowl or plastic food bag. Turn to coat meats well. Marinate 30 minutes. Remove meats and reserved marinade. Alternate ham and veal on 4 skewers, spearing a square of bell pepper on one side of each veal piece. Oil rack or spritz with nonstick cooking spray. Grill kebabs over hot fire, 10 to 15 minutes, until browned on the outside and juicy inside, turning to cook evenly. Season with salt and pepper and serve hot with rice or pasta.

GRILLED VEAL CHOP WITH LEMON AND THYME

Buy a hefty chop, an inch thick, to make veal worthwhile—no half-inchers that were breaded and panfried and cheap a generation ago. Have the fire very hot, as veal is lean and is best seared crusty brown and juicy, even a little pink, inside.

4 veal loin or rib chops, 1 inch thick, 8 ounces each

3 tablespoons lemon juice

2 tablespoons olive oil

2 tablespoons minced fresh basil leaves or
     2 teaspoons dried

Freshly ground black pepper

Salt

Lemon wedges and basil sprigs for garnish

Makes 4 large servings.

Place veal in shallow dish or large plastic food bag. Sprinkle with lemon juice, olive oil, basil, and pepper and salt to taste. Turn chops in dish or turn bag to coat with marinade. Marinate 20 to 30 minutes. Discard marinade. Brush grill with olive oil or spritz with nonstick cooking spray. Place chops on grill over very hot fire. Grill until sizzling and browned lightly. Turn and grill other side. Test with knife near center. If not done to taste, push to side of grill or close cover on grill and cook a few minutes longer. Veal is best if slightly pink at center. Salt to taste, place on hot platter, and garnish with lemon wedges and basil sprigs.

LAMB

Lamb is ideal for barbecue because of its natural tenderness and delicate flavor. Wood or charcoal smoke gives lamb special zest. I've barbecued lamb with my family in Florida, in California, and even on my apartment terrace in New York.

The mutton barbecues of western Kentucky are legendary. Alben Barkley, U.S. Senator and later Vice President, once joked that a Kentucky politician's skill at getting votes was in direct proportion to his level of eloquence after a healthy serving of barbecued mutton. Churches and men's clubs would put on the barbecues as fund-raisers, with one or two amateur chefs in charge of the cooking at each spot, and politicians would invariably come to speak to the crowds gathered for some traditional Kentucky food.

The mutton for the Kentucky barbecues is provided by local purveyors. If you find robust-flavored mutton in a market buy some, as the tender cuts are superb for grilling rare and juicy. The recipes here, however, are worked out for young lamb, easily available from good butchers and supermarkets almost everywhere.

VINEYARD BUTTERFLIED LEG OF LAMB

A leg of lamb butterflied, boned, split almost through, and opened like a book suits my style better than a whole leg (see page 88). The slab of meat is uneven, so when grilled there is always some pink inside—for me—and the thinner spots are medium or well-done. Phone ahead and ask the butcher to cut the lamb for you.

1 leg of lamb, 6 to 7 pounds, boned and butterflied

2 cloves garlic, minced

2 teaspoons curry powder

1 cup white Zinfandel or California pink or light red wine

Salt and freshly ground pepper

3 tablespoons currant or apple jelly

Makes 6 to 8 servings.

Place lamb in a shallow dish or plastic bag. In a small bowl, mix together the garlic, curry powder, wine, salt and pepper to taste, and the jelly. Beat until well blended. Pour marinade over lamb, turn to coat meat well, cover dish or close bag, and marinate 1 hour at room temperature or 3 to 4 hours in refrigerator.

Remove lamb from marinade, reserving marinade, and pat dry with paper towel. Place meat on grill over coals that are burned down until covered with gray ash. Brown lamb, brush lightly with reserved marinade, and brown other side. Cover grill or fit a loose tent of foil over lamb to hold in heat. Turn and brush with marinade every 10 to 12 minutes. Grill 30 to 40 minutes for mostly rare meat with crusty exterior, or 60 minutes for well-done. Slice and serve hot. Leftovers make good sandwiches or salads.

LAMB BARBECUE IN THE ROCKIES

A sheep grower of Greek ancestry and his handsome family did the most spectacular lamb barbecue I've ever seen. They barbecued eleven lambs in a plaza at the center of Vail, Colorado, to celebrate a bicycle race through the winding streets of the resort town, and I was invited by the lamb growers to participate. The lambs had been slaughtered and dressed the night before, then marinated overnight in a light sauce of lemon and herbs. The whole lambs were put on enormous spits—small hardwood trees freshly cut for the occasion—two lambs to the spit, except for the odd one that was on a spit alone. Two of the sheepman's dark-eyed sons hand-rotated the spits every 15 minutes or so, when the meat on one side was sizzling and browned, and they turned and basted the lamb from dawn until about 1:00 P.M., when the feast was served. The wood fires were laid in strips, like bean hills, just to the leeward side of the lamb so that the fat dripped in trenches dug below the spits. Bicycle racers were given tickets to the barbecue, while several hundred vacationers and townspeople bought tickets to share the food—freshly carved lamb piled high on trays, salads, pilaf, and good Greek bread. The sheepman's wife and daughters provided baklava, and the same daughter whom I'd seen herd several hundred sheep down a mountain the day before poured iced tea.

LAMB

BASQUE LAMB BARBECUE

The Kern County Sheepmen's Picnic in Bakersfield, California, is a joyful reunion of two or three thousand sheepmen, their families, and friends. Basque sheepherders who came to this country before the 1960s often stayed to become permanent settlers, buying a few sheep to start and gradually building their herds, and some going into other businesses. The picnic is held in late summer, usually on a blistering hot day, but it is always a gala event, with a sheep auction, dance troupes in costume that come from as far away as San Francisco, men squirting red wine from their sheepskin botas, women showing off children, and everybody eating the barbecued lamb steaks, potato salad, salsa, and chili beans. I marvel at the efficiency of the volunteer chefs who barbecue the lamb, marinating it overnight in barrels of this sauce. I have adapted their way to home-size barbecuing.

½ cup oil

½ cup wine vinegar

½ cup dry white wine

1 clove garlic, minced

½ teaspoon rubbed sage

1 teaspoon salt

¼ teaspoon freshly ground pepper

6 lamb steaks cut from the leg or shoulder, ¾ inch thick

Makes 6 servings.

In a shallow dish combine oil, vinegar, wine, garlic, sage, salt, and pepper. Add lamb and turn to coat well. Cover and marinate at room temperature 2 hours or 24 to 36 hours in the refrigerator, turning once or twice. Bring to room temperature in marinade before grilling.

Drain lamb and grill 4 inches above hot coals 8 to 10 minutes on each side or until done as desired. Lamb fat and the marinade will make the fire flare up, so have a water pistol or bottle of water nearby to extinguish flames. Basque picnic chefs serve lamb steaks with Santa Maria Salsa (see page 250), California Chili Beans (see page 219), My Grandmother's Potato Salad (see page 244), and good bread.

MINTED BUTTERFLIED LAMB

Sweet mint sauces and lamb don't appeal to me, but if fresh mint grows next to the barbecue spot, as it did in one garden a few years ago, this is a natural. The fresh sprigs nestled under the hot lamb are the ultimate aromatic splendor.

2 tablespoons olive oil
¼ cup wine vinegar
1 to 2 cloves garlic, minced
6 or 8 leafy mint sprigs, minced, or 1 teaspoon dried mint
1 leg of lamb, 5 to 6 pounds, butterflied
Mint sprigs for garnish, optional

Makes 6 to 8 servings, with leftovers.

In a small saucepan, combine oil, vinegar, and garlic. Add mint flakes, if fresh mint is unavailable. Heat until sizzling. Place lamb on grill over hot coals. Grill 30 minutes to 1 hour, until done as desired, basting often with mint sauce. Heat any remaining sauce and pour over lamb before serving.

If fresh mint is available, line warm platter with leafy sprigs and place lamb on mint. Slice lamb and serve with pilaf or baked potatoes and a big salad. Leftovers make hearty sandwiches on French rolls the next day.

TO BUTTERFLY LEG OF LAMB

If a butcher can't butterfly a leg of lamb for you, it is do-able at home, if you equip yourself with a sharp thin-bladed knife (a boning knife), a chef's knife, and chopping board.

Starting at the shank end, make a deep slit to bone, cutting toward butt end. Pull meat away from bone, cutting as needed to loosen it smoothly. Work thin knife around knobby bones. When meat is detached from bones, cut lamb almost through horizontally, then flatten by pressing with the heel of your hand.

A butterflied leg of lamb may be stuffed or folded over herbs, but for grills the flat rather uneven roast is ideal.

LAMB CHOPS WITH PEPPERS

Red peppers are used increasingly since they're imported year-round now from Holland, where they grow in hothouses, but my friend Marlene Guerry says they've been a mark of good Basque cookery for generations.

4 sweet red peppers

4 lamb chops or steaks, 1 inch thick

1/2 teaspoon garlic salt

1 teaspoon Worcestershire sauce

1 teaspoon vinegar

1 tablespoon oil

1 clove garlic, minced

2 or 3 tablespoons olive oil

Makes 4 servings.

Peppers can be prepared ahead of time and refrigerated, or frozen with a little salt and oil sprinkled over them. Spear each pepper on a fork and hold over a hot grill fire or gas flame, or place peppers in a greased shallow baking dish and bake in a very hot oven (450 degrees), until skins wrinkle. Place peppers in cold water and peel off skins. Cut out stems and remove seeds and ribs, keeping peppers whole, if possible. Have peppers at room temperature before cooking.

Rub lamb chops on both sides with garlic salt, Worcestershire sauce, vinegar, and oil. Let stand at room temperature 30 minutes.

Grill lamb 4 inches above hot coals. In a skillet at edge of grill heat minced garlic in olive oil. Add prepared peppers and sauté slowly while cooking lamb. Grill and turn lamb until done as desired, about 8 minutes on each side for rare to 12 minutes on each side for well-done. Place a pepper on each lamb chop and remove to platter.

GRILL–ROASTED LAMB

Lamb turned on a spit reminds me of gargantuan Elizabethan feasts, when meat was meat and royalty ate it. Spit instructions are here, but many experienced chefs prefer roasting big pieces of meat by indirect heat on the grill. Remember, balancing a leg of lamb with bone in is tricky.

1 leg of lamb, 5 to 6 pounds
2 cloves garlic, slivered
½ cup dry white wine
1 bay leaf, crumbled with rib removed
1 green pepper, chopped fine
½ teaspoon dried thyme
½ teaspoon salt
¼ teaspoon freshly ground pepper
¼ cup olive oil

Makes 8 to 10 servings.

Have lamb shank removed or folded back under roast. Pierce fat side of roast with tip of knife and poke in slivers of garlic. Place lamb in deep plastic bag. In bowl, combine wine, bay leaf, green pepper, thyme, salt, and pepper. Beat to dissolve seasonings. Beat in olive oil. Pour over lamb, seal bag, and turn to coat meat well. Marinate several hours or overnight in refrigerator, turning bag every hour or so, except during night. Drain lamb, reserving marinade.

To roast by indirect heat: Start fire 30 to 45 minutes before grilling. When fire has burned to hot coals covered with gray ash, push coals with poker to one side or into circle to surround drip pan. (In gas grill fire need be lighted only 15 minutes before cooking, and in two-burner grill light only one side, to allow space for drip pan on other side.) Use disposable foil pan or wrap kitchen pan in foil to protect from smoke and push beside or among coals. Place lamb over drip pan. Cover grill or shape a loose tent of foil over lamb and coals to hold in heat. Roast 1½ to 2½ hours, to 125 degrees for rare, to 160 degrees for well-done. Baste periodically with reserved marinade.

To spit roast: Build fire and position drip pan under space where spitted meat will turn. While fire is burning down, position lamb on spit. Thrust spit point lengthwise and diagonally through leg, keeping weight balanced. Push spit forks in firmly to hold meat steady. Engage spit and start turning. Stop spit motor and baste meat every 15 minutes. Cover is not closed when rotisserie is operating. Roast 1¼ to 2 hours, to doneness desired. Stop motor and baste meat with reserved marinade every 15 to 20 minutes.

To serve grill-roasted leg of lamb, place on platter or board. Crimp foil closely around it and let stand 20 to 30 minutes before carving. Carve and serve hot.

Pan drippings can be used for a simple sauce. Carefully remove drip pan from firebox. Skim as much fat as possible off, using a bulb baster or spoon. Mince a small shallot or 2 or 3 scallions and sauté in skillet rubbed with oil until translucent. Stir in pan drippings and ¼ cup minced fresh thyme and salt and pepper to taste. Simmer a minute or 2 and spoon over hot meat.

A NAPA VALLEY LAMB BARBEQUE

We once drove up the Napa Valley on a summer afternoon when grapes were filling out to hang heavy on the vines for the harvest a few weeks later. Stopping to buy a few bottles of wine, we noticed the heavy aroma of barbecuing lamb in the air. I followed my nose and found the winegrower's wife basting lamb with a sauce so simple that lamb remains the main taste: white Zinfandel, garlic, curry powder, and a few spoonfuls of currant jelly for sweetening. White Zinfandel, which really is pale to deep pink, has become almost a pop wine, but seems to have more character than conventional rosés and pink "luncheon" wines. In fact, white Zinfandel or light red ones are a good choice with barbecue.

GRILLED LAMB CHOPS WITH MINT

Dried mint flakes season well, if used within a few months of purchase and kept tightly closed and away from heat. But fresh mint clipped when the dew is on it in the morning has a fine flavor, too.

8 loin or rib lamb chops, 1½ inches thick

1 tablespoon dried mint flakes or minced fresh mint leaves

2 tablespoons red wine vinegar

Salt and freshly ground pepper

Makes 6 servings.

Place chops in shallow dish and sprinkle with mint and vinegar. Marinate at room temperature for 30 minutes to 1 hour. Remove chops from marinade, shaking off as much sauce as possible. Place chops on grill over hot coals. Grill until browned, turn, and brown other side. Continue grilling and turning until done as desired, 15 to 18 minutes for medium-rare, 25 minutes for well-done. Sprinkle with salt and pepper and serve hot.

ROSEMARY LAMB CHOPS

Rosemary is planted on hillsides in Southern California to discourage flower-eating deer from invading gardens. This herb grows easily in almost any sunny spot, as we discovered our first summer in North Carolina. It is a great joy to pluck a few sprigs to flavor lamb chops or any number of other foods.

6 rib or loin lamb chops, 1½ inches thick
6 large sprigs fresh or dried rosemary
Olive oil
Salt and freshly ground pepper

Makes 6 servings.

Place chops on grill over hot coals and place a sprig of rosemary on each or sprinkle lightly with dried rosemary. Brush with oil and grill until browned. Turn, moving fresh rosemary to rest on grill underneath chops, and brown other side. Dried rosemary will cling to chops when turned. Grill and turn, basting with more oil as needed to keep moist, until lamb is done as desired, 15 to 18 minutes for medium-rare, 25 minutes for well-done. Sprinkle with salt and pepper and serve hot.

MIXED GRILL KEBABS

In Turkish and East Indian cookery, shish kebab means meat grilled on skewers, usually with vegetables. The meat is heavily spiced and when you walk along the streets in Istanbul and other Middle Eastern cities you can smell an exotic blend of spices from street grills or wafting from people's kitchens.

This gourmand's version of shish kebab was invented by my late husband Luther by adding one idea to another until he had the most mixed-up skewerful of meat I've ever seen. It was a favorite summertime party dish, since the only accompaniment you needed was bread to sop up the meat and vegetable juices.

1½ pounds leg of lamb, cut in 1½-inch cubes

1 pound boneless tender sirloin of beef,
    cut in 1½-inch cubes

¼ cup oil

½ cup dry red wine

2 tablespoons wine vinegar

½ teaspoon thyme

2 tablespoons minced scallions or shallots

12 to 18 mushroom caps

12 small whole onions, about 1 pound

¾ pound calf's liver, cut in 1-inch cubes

About ½ pound bacon

2 green peppers, seeded and cut in 1-inch squares

Salt and freshly ground pepper

Makes 6 servings.

In a large bowl combine lamb, beef, oil, wine, vinegar, thyme, and scallions or shallots. Mix well. Cover and marinate in refrigerator 4 hours or longer, stirring several times with a spoon. Simmer mushrooms about 2 minutes in boiling water to prevent splitting when threading on skewers. Cut off ends of onions and simmer onions in water 5 minutes or until skins slip off easily; then slip off skins. Wrap cubes of liver in a half strip of bacon each.

Drain lamb and beef, reserving marinade. Alternate lamb, beef, and bacon-wrapped liver with vegetables on 6 skewers. Refrigerate until ready to cook.

Grill 3 to 4 inches above hot coals 25 to 30 minutes, basting with reserved marinade as needed and turning to cook evenly. This produces medium-rare meat with the bacon crisp. Push off onto warm plates, serving 1 skewer per person (though a few strong souls will claim they can't eat that much, they usually do).

GREEK LAMB KEBABS

Lamb grilled on pushcart charcoal firepots is a fond memory of many tourists who have visited Athens and the Greek islands. You also see Greek-style lamb kebabs sold on the streets of New York, the skewerful of meat served with a pita bread.

2 pounds lean, well-trimmed leg of lamb,
    cut in 1½-inch cubes
¼ cup each rich-flavored olive oil and lemon juice
15 to 20 bay leaves
1 teaspoon crumbled oregano
½ teaspoon salt
Freshly ground pepper to taste
2 onions, cut in wedges

Makes 6 servings.

Place lamb in a plastic bag or dish. In a small bowl combine olive oil and lemon juice, 2 bay leaves finely crumbled, the oregano, salt, and pepper. Pour over lamb, mix well, and let marinate at room temperature about 1 hour. Drain meat well, reserving marinade. Thread lamb and onion pieces on skewers, spearing a bay leaf between pieces of meat and onion here and there.

Grill 4 to 5 inches from hot coals, basting occasionally with the reserved marinade, until done as desired, about 15 minutes for medium-rare. Push meat off skewers and serve hot.

SKEWER TRICKS

For more rare meat, jam meat close together on skewers. If you like crispy edges, and more well-done meat, allow space between chunks of meat.

Spear onions, mushrooms, whole plum or cherry tomatoes, and bell pepper diagonally to prevent splitting; a few will split anyway. Save the discards for omelet, soup, or whatever you like tomorrow. Steaming mushrooms for a few minutes before threading them on skewers prevents splitting, too.

KOFTA KEBABS

Kofta is a fine-textured dense meatball typical of eastern Mediterranean cooking. Traditionally vigorous kneading of the meat has produced the firm texture of the meat. Although I learned from Armenian friends in California how to knead the meat by hand, I have found that a food processor not only works as well but is faster.

2 small onions, cut in chunks

2 cloves garlic, smashed

2 eggs

1 teaspoon cinnamon

1 teaspoon salt

Freshly ground pepper to taste

2 pounds ground lean lamb (see Note page 103)

Fine dry bread crumbs

Makes 5 or 6 servings.

To prepare by hand, finely chop onions and garlic and knead thoroughly into meat with eggs and seasonings. To prepare in food processor, put onions in processor fitted with steel blade and finely chop. Add garlic, eggs, cinnamon, salt, and pepper and process until well blended. Add lamb and process until pasty, once or twice turning motor off and scraping side of container. Chill well.

Gather up hunks of meat mixture about the size of golf balls, flatten, and sprinkle 1 side with bread crumbs. Shape, crumbed side in, around flat skewers and coat outside of kebabs with crumbs. Place kebabs in well-greased hinged wire grill, arranging so skewers don't slip through wires.

Grill 3 to 4 inches above hot coals until browned; turn and brown other side. Allow 10 minutes each side for well-done, 6 to 8 minutes for rare to medium. Serve on a bed of flat-leaf parsley with rice and a salad of mixed greens, finely chopped parsley, tomato, cucumber, diced sweet red and green pepper, and onion.

ARMENIAN SHISH KEBABS

Armenian friends in California taught me to cook vegetables on skewers separate from meat so that the vegetables don't break apart and fall into the fire before the meat is done. My friend Nectar Avakian seasoned her meat and vegetables lightly and simply for superb kebabs.

3 pounds boneless leg of lamb, cut in 1½-inch cubes

½ cup dry red wine

2 tablespoons olive oil

½ teaspoon dried mint flakes or 2 tablespoons
    minced fresh mint

2 cloves garlic, minced

6 to 8 plum tomatoes

2 large sweet green or red peppers, quartered

2 medium onions, quartered

2 large zucchini, about 6 ounces each, cut in 4 chunks each

Salt and freshly ground pepper

Makes 6 generous servings.

In bowl, combine lamb with wine, oil, mint, and garlic. Mix with your hands and spoon. Cover and marinate 30 minutes at room temperature or 4 hours in refrigerator, turning once or twice. Drain lamb, reserving marinade and juices that have collected. Thread on skewers. Thread tomatoes, pepper, and onion pieces diagonally on other skewers and zucchini on another skewer.

Grill lamb over hot coals 10 minutes. Place vegetable kebabs on grill, with peppers and onions near hottest part of fire, zucchini next, and tomatoes near edge of grill. Brush meat and vegetables with reserved marinade. Turn and grill lamb until almost done, about 5 minutes longer, and push off skewers into a large pot set at edge of grill to keep lamb hot while finishing vegetables. Continue to cook and baste until vegetables are done as desired. Onions and peppers require 18 to 20 minutes, zucchini, 10 minutes, and tomatoes, 8 to 10 minutes.

To serve, pile lamb cubes in center of a large platter. Push vegetables off skewers and arrange around meat for colorful display. Serve hot with pilaf or potato salad. The typical Armenian salad served with shish kebab includes more of the same vegetables—chopped tomato, green bell peppers, and onion—plus a handful of minced parsley, salad greens, and lemon and oil dressing.

BINGHAMTON SPIEDIES

The overnight marinating and cutting meat in small cubes allows use of less tender cuts.

2 teaspoons *each* salt and black pepper

1 teaspoon *each* paprika and parsley flakes

1 tablespoon dried oregano leaves

¼ teaspoon rosemary leaves

1 large clove garlic, minced

2 medium onions, chopped fine

¼ cup red wine vinegar

1½ cups olive or vegetable oil

2 pounds boneless lamb shoulder, beef top round or
　　chuck, pork shoulder or loin, or venison chuck, cut in
　　1-inch cubes

Makes

4 to 6

servings.

Combine seasonings, garlic, and onions in blender or food processor with vinegar and oil. Mix thoroughly. Pour over meat in large plastic bag. Close bag, turn, and manipulate bag to distribute marinade. Place in bowl and marinate 24 hours, turning bag now and then.

Drain marinade and thread meat on skewers. Grill over hot coals until done as desired, 15 to 20 minutes. Test pork with fork to see that juices run clear. Serve hot with rice or potatoes.

Note: Excess marinade can be refrigerated or frozen and used for later batches of spiedies.

VICE PRESIDENT BRECKINRIDGE AT A BARBECUE
"Old Crow is present" on this and similar occasions, when such noted Kentuckians as "General John C. Breckinridge, Senator James B. Beck, Senator Joe Blackburn, or the Governor of the state," gather for a day of political oratory, roast sheep and mint juleps.*
*From the Memoirs of Henry F. Johnson.

ITALIAN BARBECUE, UPPER NEW YORK STYLE

Upper New York State has contributed two Italian novelties to the American table, spiedies and pizza.

During World War II the glories of "tomato pie from Buffalo" were spread by folk from the East. In the fifties pizza mixes were in every home and most families were within driving distance of a pizza parlor. Shortly afterward, tourists found pizza in Italy. Italians had viewed it as a snack unworthy of the tourist trade.

In the early eighties I discovered spiedies in Binghamton, New York. My friend Elaine Montgomery tells me she grew up with them. She and her high school chums stopped at the spiedie cafe after school to indulge, as teenagers do. The herbed oniony marinade is a delicious memory to her.

The originator of spiedies went out of business, but the skewered meat lives on in other restaurants and on backyard grills. Lamb was the original meat, but homefolk offer chicken, beef, and pork spiedies, as well as lamb.

Many food observers assume the name is a corruption of *spedini,* appetizer sandwiches skewered and grilled. And nobody disputes it. It is worth a try some lazy weekend when you have time to marinate the meat.

LAMB SHANKS WITH PINEAPPLE AND PEPPERS

Lamb shanks should be partially cooked before barbecuing to insure tenderness and remove some of the fat. The shanks can be flavored with almost any good barbecue sauce, but they are especially tasty with fresh pineapple and sweet peppers, as here.

4 small lamb shanks, ¾ pound each
Salt and freshly ground pepper
1 clove garlic, minced
1 small onion, grated or minced
½ cup oil
⅓ cup beef or chicken broth
¾ cup pineapple juice
4 thick slices fresh pineapple, peeled and cored
1 large or 2 small green peppers, seeded and quartered

Makes 4 servings.

Preheat oven to 400 degrees. Place each lamb shank on a square of aluminum foil, season lightly with salt and pepper, wrap tightly, and place in a shallow baking dish. Bake until lamb is tender, about 40 minutes. Open packets and pour off fat. Rewrap and place in a plastic food bag and refrigerate or freeze; or lamb can be cooked immediately.

Bring lamb to room temperature. In a bowl beat together garlic, onion, oil, broth, and pineapple juice. Pour into a plastic bag or dish. Unwrap lamb shanks and add, turning to coat with sauce. Marinate 1 hour at room temperature or 4 hours in refrigerator. Drain lamb, reserving marinade.

Grill lamb and pineapple over hot coals, brushing once or twice with reserved marinade and turning to brown and cook evenly. After 15 minutes, add pepper wedges and brush with sauce. Lamb and pineapple require 25 to 30 minutes' cooking, and peppers, 10 minutes. Arrange lamb, pineapple, and peppers on a platter.

LAMBURGERS ON BUNS

Chutney, mustard, mint or cranberry jelly, or other condiments may be added to this simple burger, but my taste is for the clean flavor of lamb perked lightly with lemon juice on a buttered bun with tomato and onion.

1½ pounds lean ground lamb (see Note, page 103)

1 clove garlic, minced

½ teaspoon salt

¼ teaspoon freshly ground pepper

1 tablespoon lemon juice

4 sandwich buns, split and toasted lightly on grill

Butter

Sliced tomato and onion

Makes 4 servings.

Lightly mix lamb, garlic, salt, pepper, and lemon juice. Shape into 4 patties about 1 inch thick.

Grill over hot coals until done as desired, turning to cook evenly and prevent burning. Total cooking time for rare is about 12 minutes; for medium, 15 minutes; and for well-done, 18 to 20 minutes.

Butter buns, place hot lamb patty on bottom half of each, then top with tomato, onion, and other half of bun.

GRILLED BONED LAMB SHOULDER ROAST

Boned and rolled lamb shoulder roast is available in some areas. If your meat man does not show it regularly, order ahead, and you'll be glad you made the effort. This cut is juicy, full-flavored, and many lamb lovers think it tastier than leg of lamb. It is compact, so it is easy to carve.

1 lamb shoulder, boned, rolled, and tied, 3 to 4 pounds

2 cups beef or chicken broth

¼ cup soy sauce

2 cloves garlic, minced

1 tablespoon grated orange peel or diced dried peel

Few drops hot pepper sauce

Makes 6 to 8 servings.

Place lamb in plastic bag or deep bowl. Mix broth, soy sauce, garlic, orange peel, and pepper sauce. Pour over lamb, turn to coat well, and marinate at room temperature 1 hour or in refrigerator 4 to 6 hours. Drain lamb, reserving marinade. Push hot coals to back or in large circle to allow placement of drip pan. Place disposable foil or kitchen pan wrapped in foil to protect it from smoke into spot below cooking area. Place lamb over drip pan.

Grill 2 to 2½ hours, turning and basting with marinade from time to time. Cook to 130 degrees for rare; 150 degrees for medium-rare; and 160 for well-done. Let lamb stand 15 to 20 minutes and carve.

BARBECUED STUFFED BREAST OF LAMB

1 lamb breast rack, 1½ to 2 pounds
1 pound ground lean lamb
2 cloves garlic, minced
2 tablespoons minced fresh or 2 teaspoons
    dried rosemary
Salt and freshly ground pepper
Dry red wine

*Makes 4
servings.*

Have lamb breast cut with a pocket so it can be stuffed. Mix ground lamb with garlic, 1 teaspoon rosemary, ¼ teaspoon salt, and pepper to taste. Push lamb mixture firmly into pocket of lamb breast. This will form a compact triangle of meat with a bony side and a meaty side and ground lamb forming the longest side of the triangle. (Some markets prepare lamb breast with meat stuffing, but it will not be seasoned.) Before cooking, sprinkle remaining rosemary over lamb.

Place lamb breast bony side down over moderately hot coals. Have a spritzer handy to extinguish any flare-ups. Sprinkle meat with red wine now and then. When bony side is browned, turn the roast to meaty side of the breast and grill until browned. By this time the ground meat filling will be firm. Turn filling down toward coals and grill until done as desired. Total grilling time for medium-rare lamb will be about 1 hour. Cut through lamb breast between bones to form triangular slices for serving. (Kitchen shears cut through bones and connective tissue more easily than a knife.)

Note: Buy 2 pounds lamb shoulder, cut out bone and most of the visible fat and sinew, and put through meat grinder or process with steel blade in food processor.

GRILLED LAMB KIDNEYS

Breakfast on the terrace or in the back yard is a joyous spring Sunday tradition. Should you awaken one morning to warm sunshine and are prepared with lamb kidneys on hand, let them become the centerpiece of your breakfast. One spring Sunday we scrambled eggs in a skillet at the edge of the grill and toasted thick slices of sourdough bread to go with the kidneys. The bread was buttered generously and served with homemade strawberry preserves. We had fresh apricots off the back yard tree for fruit.

6 to 8 lamb kidneys

2 tablespoons olive oil

1 tablespoon red wine vinegar

1/2 teaspoon thyme

1/2 teaspoon freshly ground pepper

6 slices bacon, cut in squares

Makes 6 servings, with eggs or bacon or ham.

Wash lamb kidneys; split them and remove fat and any tough sinewy portions. Place in plastic bag; add oil, vinegar, thyme, and pepper and marinate at room temperature 10 to 15 minutes. Thread kidneys lengthwise or slightly diagonally on short skewers, placing a square of bacon between each piece.

Brush with marinade and grill 3 to 4 inches from hot fire until browned. Turn and grill other side. Slip off skewers onto warm plates and serve at once.

CHICKEN AND TURKEY

Barbecuing gives character to the mild-flavored chickens and turkeys that agricultural science has brought to our markets. These young things are sure to be tender, if you avoid overcooking them. A broiler-fryer slaughtered at eight to nine weeks can't compare with the matronly birds that my grandmother called "spring chickens."

A chicken barbecue is a traditional American feast. Some town squares in the South still have "pits," which really stand aboveground. A rectangular cinder-block structure about waist high for the chief cooks, three feet wide and twelve to twenty feet long, has a wire grill (usually made by a local blacksmith or handyman) set three or four inches below the top rim. In the fifties and sixties the town barbecue was a summer event. Women brought salads, coleslaw, or fresh sweet corn to drop into the corn-boil pot and the whole town ate in community harmony.

And everybody barbecued chicken at home. Just don't cook it too fast and or too long or those tender little birds become tough and dry.

Turkey parts and cutlets open up a whole new world of great barbecue food. The marketing revolution that switched turkey from holiday bird to summer feast was just beginning when we moved to California in 1960. It took a few years, but now more interesting turkey cuts are available in the summer than around holiday times. And a whole small turkey roasted on a grill remains festive. Each year RV owners rendezvous in Death Valley for Thanksgiving, many cooks bringing along traditional foods, and the turkey is roasted on a covered grill, brought along for the feast.

BARBECUED CHICKEN QUARTERS

Choose any sauce you like, but the Florida Barbecue Sauce reminds me of town barbecues of a generation ago. One quarter of a chicken will make a medium-size serving—half a chicken a very generous one.

3 broiler-fryers, quartered, 3 pounds each
Florida Barbecue Sauce (page 192), or sauce
    of your choice

*Makes
6 to 12
servings.*

Place chicken, skin side down, over hot fire. Cook 10 minutes or until skin side is browned, turn, and baste with sauce. Brown bony side. Brush sparingly with sauce, turning and basting every time fire begins to leap up. Total grilling time will be 45 minutes to 1 hour. Heat remaining sauce and serve on the side.

TEXAS BARBECUED CHICKEN

Jane Cherry never lost her Texas accent or her hand at barbecuing in the years that she and Heston lived in Los Angeles, where her cooking was famed. They've moved back to College Station, and she recommends this chicken hot or cold with a huge tray of fruit salad for a summer meal.

1 broiler-fryer, 3 pounds, quartered
Basic Dry Rub (page 189)
Texas Barbecue Sauce (page 194)

*Makes 4
servings.*

Rub chicken generously with seasoning. Place on grill over hot coals and grill until browned, turn, and brown other side. Continue to turn and grill for 15 to 20 minutes, then brush with sauce and grill 10 minutes longer, turning once or twice and basting lightly with sauce. Heat remaining sauce and pass at table with chicken.

TWO–SAUCE CHICKEN

Chicken prepared this way turns a rich mahogany color, but does not burn if you keep extinguishing any flames with a convenient water bottle. The first sauce gives the chicken a pale tawny color; the second brings it to a reddish gold.

3 broiler-fryers, split, or 2, quartered,
       2 to 2½ pounds each
2 cups vinegar
2 teaspoons salt
3 tablespoons prepared mustard, preferably Dijon-style
3 tablespoons catsup
⅓ cup lemon juice
½ teaspoon freshly ground pepper
¼ cup sugar
5⅓ tablespoons (⅓ cup) butter, melted
1 tablespoon Worcestershire sauce

Makes

6 to 8

servings.

Place chicken in a large dish or in 2 plastic bags. Combine vinegar, 1 teaspoon salt, 1 tablespoon mustard, the catsup, lemon juice, and pepper. Pour over chicken and turn chicken in marinade. Cover and refrigerate overnight.

For second sauce combine sugar, remaining 1 teaspoon salt, butter, remaining 2 tablespoons mustard, and Worcestershire sauce. Set aside.

Remove chicken from marinade and place bony side down 4 to 6 inches above hot coals. Grill 5 minutes, turn, and baste with marinade until starting to brown, about 20 minutes. Grill 30 minutes longer, turning once or twice and basting lightly with the second sauce. Test for doneness and remove to platter. Serve hot with remaining butter sauce.

SOUTHERN MUSTARD CHICKEN

Barbecue chefs, except Texans, overlook the flavor-enforcing benefit of rich chicken broth. The chicken tastes richer and broth, from which the fat has been skimmed, moistens the birds without causing flames.

¼ cup vegetable oil or butter

8 meaty chicken pieces (breasts, thighs, drumsticks)

1½ cups well-seasoned chicken broth

¼ cup Dijon-style mustard

Makes 4 servings.

Heat oil or butter in small saucepan at edge of grill. Place chicken over medium-hot coals, brush lightly with oil, reserving remainder. Grill until browned. Stir chicken broth and mustard into oil remaining in saucepan and heat. When chicken browns, turn and brush chicken generously with broth mixture. Grill, turn, and baste each time chicken browns. Total cooking time will be 30 to 45 minutes. Heat remaining sauce and serve at table with hot chicken.

JAPANESE–FLAVOR BARBECUED CHICKEN

This clean-flavored chicken is complemented by baked or fried sliced yams and a green vegetable such as broccoli.

½ cup sake or dry sherry

½ cup soy sauce

2 tablespoons honey

1 teaspoon freshly ground pepper

1 broiler-fryer, 2½ pounds, quartered

Makes 4 servings.

In stainless steel or enamelware saucepan combine sake or sherry, soy sauce, honey, and pepper. Simmer 15 minutes. Place chicken in plastic bag and marinate at room temperature 30 minutes. Remove chicken and reserve marinade. Place chicken over hot coals. Grill over hot coals, turning and basting with reserved marinade every 15 minutes until glazed, dark brown, and juices run clear when bird is pierced with fork at thick thigh joints. Serve hot.

BARBECUED MUSTARD CHICKEN

The flavors here could come straight from the Rhone Valley, but the chicken barbecue scheme is pure Californian—winy flavored, delicately spiced and sweetened.

1 cup dry white wine (California Chardonnay or white
    table wine)
½ cup olive oil
½ teaspoon salt
½ teaspoon freshly ground pepper
1 teaspoon herbes de Provence, or ½ teaspoon oregano
1 broiler-fryer, quartered, 3 pounds
1 tablespoon Dijon-style mustard
1 tablespoon honey

Makes 4 servings.

In a bowl beat together wine, oil, salt, pepper, and herbs or oregano. Place chicken in a bowl or plastic bag and add marinade. Marinate at room temperature 30 minutes, agitating chicken now and then to coat it with the sauce. Drain chicken, reserving marinade.

Grill chicken over hot fire, turning and basting as needed to cook evenly and prevent charring. Chicken will require 35 to 40 minutes' cooking. Combine 2 tablespoons remaining marinade with the mustard and honey. Brush over chicken and grill over coals until glazed and fragrant.

YOGURT CHICKEN

In India chicken marinated in yogurt and spices is barbecued in a tandoori oven, a cylinder-shaped stone chamber heated from below by a wood fire. This recipe, for a conventional charcoal grill, borrows the exotic seasonings of tandoori chicken. The yogurt distributes the spices through the chicken and is an effective tenderizer. Meat marinated this way will be butter-tender without being dry or mushy.

1 cup plain yogurt

2 cloves garlic, minced

1 small onion, finely chopped

1½ teaspoons coriander seeds, cracked

1 teaspoon ground cumin

2 teaspoons turmeric

1 teaspoon minced fresh mint, or pinch dried
     mint flakes

1 broiler-fryer, quartered, 2 to 2½ pounds each

Makes 4 servings.

Mix yogurt, garlic, onion, coriander, cumin, turmeric, and mint. Place chicken in a shallow dish or plastic bag and spread with yogurt marinade. The marinade will be thick. Cover or tie bag closed and let stand in refrigerator 8 to 12 hours, turning bag or chicken now and then. Scrape off loose onion and excess marinade into a small saucepan.

Grill chicken over hot coals; brush with more marinade as needed and turn to cook evenly. Cook just until tender and golden, 40 minutes for a medium chicken.

Note: This chicken can be cooked in a kitchen. Bake the chicken at 400 degrees in a shallow baking dish, turning and basting until done, about 35 minutes.

BARBECUED CHICKEN WITH SWEET POTATOES

This style of chicken is popular for parties in California and Florida.

½ cup pineapple juice
½ cup catsup
2 tablespoons cider vinegar
1 tablespoon honey
2 or 3 dashes hot pepper sauce
1 tablespoon prepared yellow mustard
3 broiler-fryers, 2 to 2½ pounds, quartered
2 to 3 tablespoons vegetable oil
6 large sweet potatoes

Makes 12 medium-size or 6 large servings.

Combine pineapple juice, catsup, vinegar, honey, pepper sauce, and mustard. Mix well. Place chicken in large plastic bag or shallow dish and pour sauce over it, turn well, and marinate at room temperature 30 to 45 minutes or in refrigerator 3 or 4 hours.

Remove chicken and reserve marinade. Brush chicken lightly with oil and place over hot coals. Grill until lightly browned, turning as needed to brown evenly. Meanwhile, peel sweet potatoes and cut lengthwise in slabs ½ inch thick. Place potatoes on oiled grill around chicken. Brush chicken and sweet potatoes lightly with sauce and grill about 35 minutes, until chicken is done and sweet potatoes are tender. Turn and baste every 7 to 8 minutes while cooking. Serve hot with tossed green salad or coleslaw.

GINGER CHICKEN

Ground dried ginger is a weak-kneed substitute for fresh ginger, so get the fresh if at all possible. You'll miss it if you don't have it.

¼ cup dry vermouth

¼ cup soy sauce

¼ cup molasses or dark brown sugar

¼ teaspoon freshly ground pepper

1 tablespoon grated fresh ginger root

1 broiler-fryer, quartered, 2½ pounds

Makes 4 servings.

Combine vermouth, soy sauce, molasses or brown sugar, pepper, and ginger. Place chicken in plastic bag, add marinade, close bag, and turn to coat chicken well. Marinate at room temperature 30 to 45 minutes or in refrigerator 3 to 4 hours, turning now and then. Drain chicken, reserving marinade. Grill over hot coals, turning and basting with marinade as needed to cook evenly and prevent burning. Total grilling time will be about 45 minutes. Serve hot with rice and stir-fried snow peas.

GINGER KEEPER

Ginger is used in tiny amounts in most recipes, but leftovers are easily kept for next time around.

Ginger freezes successfully and the frozen ginger can be grated easily. I peel ginger before freezing and wrap it tightly in plastic wrap and drop it in a sandwich bag with other small items (packets of tomato paste, etc.) that tend to get lost in the jumble.

Or peel and cut up ginger. Put it in a jar, cover with sherry or vodka, and keep it in the refrigerator. When the ginger is used up the spirits can be used to flavor punch or brighten several cups of hot tea.

BUTTERFLIED CHICKEN WITH LEMON AND THYME

1 broiler-fryer, about 3½ pounds
1 large lemon, halved
3 sprigs fresh or ½ teaspoon dried thyme
Olive oil
Lemon wedges, fresh thyme, or parsley

Makes 4 servings.

Ask your butcher to butterfly a chicken for you, or do it yourself with poultry or kitchen shears and a sharp knife. Place the chicken on a cutting board or heavy paper to protect the counter. With good shears cut as close to the backbone as possible from tail to neck cavity. Cut away backbone at other side and pull it out. (The backbone, wing tips, and other trimmings can be frozen for making soup or stock.) Cut any sharp bone edges or ragged pieces of skin to smooth the edge. Flatten the chicken with the heel of your hand, then smack it hard over the breastbone, which is surrounded by translucent cartilage. Cut the filament that covers the breastbone, then turn the chicken inside out and pull out the breastbone. Butterflying the chicken allows the meat to cook evenly and makes carving neat slices easier.

Place chicken in a plastic bag and squeeze the lemon over it. Rub lemon into fleshy pieces. Sprinkle chicken with thyme. Close bag and marinate chicken at room temperature 45 minutes or in the refrigerator for several hours. Turn the bag 2 or 3 times to distribute juices and seasonings.

Remove chicken from bag and place skin side up on grill 5 inches above hot coals. Brush generously with oil and cook until browned; turn and brush with oil and cook until browned. Move chicken to edge of grill or cover grill and cook 35 minutes longer or until chicken is tender and golden brown.

Meanwhile, in a small saucepan heat 2 to 3 tablespoons oil and the remaining lemon-thyme mixture. Brush over chicken and transfer to a hot platter. Garnish with lemon wedges and fresh thyme or parsley, if available. Slice to serve.

SOY–HONEY GLAZED CHICKEN BREASTS

Chicken glazed with sweet-savory sauces such as this can be broiled, but charcoal cooking enhances the flavor. Cook the chicken just until done through to prevent drying out.

2 chicken breasts, split, 1 pound each

1/4 cup minced scallions

2 cloves garlic, pressed

1 tablespoon honey

2 tablespoons dry sherry

2 teaspoons grated fresh ginger root (optional)

1/2 cup soy sauce

Makes 4 servings.

Skin chicken breast pieces. Combine scallions, garlic, honey, sherry, ginger root, and soy sauce. Dip chicken in sauce, then place in plastic bag and pour in remaining sauce. Close bag and marinate at room temperature 30 minutes to 1 hour.

Grill over hot coals, turning as needed to prevent charring and to cook evenly. Grill until just done, about 25 minutes. Brush with sauce as needed to keep moist. Heat any remaining sauce and serve with chicken and hot cooked rice.

WHITE LEGHORNS,
Bred by C.A.Pitkin, Hartford.Conn.

YAKITORI

This Americanized version of a Japanese dish goes fast as party food. Serve two of the little skewers as an entree.

3 whole chicken breasts, skinned and boned, or
      1½-pounds breast fillets, cut in 1-inch cubes
½ cup sake or dry sherry
½ cup soy sauce
1 tablespoon sugar
1 clove garlic, crushed
12 bamboo skewers
2 green or red bell peppers, cut in squares
1 medium onion, cut in 8 wedges

Makes 12 appetizer or 4 to 6 main-dish servings.

Place chicken cubes in plastic bag. Mix together sake or sherry, soy sauce, sugar, and garlic. Stir to dissolve sugar and pour over chicken. Close bag, turn to coat chicken, and marinate 3 to 4 hours in refrigerator. Soak skewers in water for 1 hour. Drain marinade into small saucepan and heat at edge of grill. Thread chicken pieces, pepper, and onion on skewers with pepper and onion pieces interspersed between chicken. Grill on hibachi or other small hot fire turning once or twice for 4 to 5 minutes.

CARIBBEAN FLAVOR CHICKEN

Adobo seasoning is around many places, as retailers recognize the good things that Caribbean cookery offers and the fact that Hispanics are good food buyers. I sometimes use the bottled seasoning in this recipe in place of the salt, garlic, oregano, paprika, and lemon juice.

1 teaspoon salt

1 clove garlic, peeled, plus 2 cloves, minced

1½ teaspoons dried leaf oregano

¼ teaspoon paprika

1 tablespoon lemon or lime juice

8 meaty chicken pieces (breasts, thighs, drumsticks)

3 tablespoons oil

1 small onion, minced

⅓ cup catsup

⅓ cup cider vinegar

Makes 4 servings.

With a mortar and pestle or with back of spoon against bowl, mash salt with peeled garlic to a paste. Work in ½ teaspoon oregano, the paprika, and lemon juice. Rub this mixture over chicken. Brush with 1 tablespoon oil.

Place chicken over hot coals and grill, turning every 7 to 8 minutes, until done. Meanwhile, sauté onion in remaining 2 tablespoons oil until tender. Add minced garlic and sauté a few seconds. Stir in catsup, vinegar, and remaining oregano and simmer 15 minutes. When chicken is done brush with sauce and grill 5 minutes longer. Pile onto a warm platter and serve remaining sauce at table. Fried plantains or bananas baked on the grill or saffron rice go well with this.

CHICKEN THIGHS WITH PESTO

Fresh basil has become a national passion. It grows in many an herb bed, and a friend who lives in a New York apartment has it in a pot on her bedroom windowsill. One night I had some leftover pesto and I tried it as a sauce for grilled chicken thighs.

Chicken thighs are first choice for barbecuing because they are meaty and juicier than other chicken parts. The pesto contributes a rich herby flavor that makes this a savory dish, especially when accompanied by rice cooked in chicken broth and a big green salad tossed with an olive oil and balsamic vinegar dressing.

⅓ cup oil

⅓ cup Pesto (recipe follows)

12 chicken thighs

Additional Pesto

Makes 6 servings.

In a shallow dish combine oil and pesto, beating with fork until well mixed. Dip chicken thighs in sauce, turn, and cover. Let stand at room temperature 30 minutes.

Grill chicken over hot coals, basting once or twice with sauce. Cook and turn until done, about 35 minutes. Heat remaining sauce to serve with chicken at table. Pass additional Pesto, at room temperature, if you wish.

PESTO

2 cups fresh basil leaves, loosely packed

2 cloves garlic, smashed

¼ cup walnuts or pine nuts

½ to ¾ cup olive oil

½ cup freshly grated Parmesan cheese

¼ teaspoon salt, or to taste

Makes about 1 cup.

In a blender or processor combine basil, garlic, nuts, and ½ cup oil. Process until almost smooth. If pasty, add more oil. Scrape into a bowl and beat in cheese and salt to taste. Serve as a sauce on pasta or rice or use as a flavoring for vegetable soup, as well as in sauce for Chicken Thighs with Pesto.

GRILLED CHICKEN GIBLETS

Chicken giblets are snatched almost faster than you can cook them when guests are hanging around the grill.

½ teaspoon salt

½ teaspoon freshly ground pepper

½ teaspoon sugar

½ teaspoon dried leaf sage

2 tablespoons wine vinegar or lemon juice

⅓ cup olive oil

Livers, hearts, and gizzards from 3 broiler-fryers

Makes appe- tizers for 6 persons.

In small bowl mix salt, pepper, sugar, and sage. Stir in vinegar or juice until well mixed. Beat in oil. Let stand while preparing giblets. Rinse giblets and cut away cartilage or fat. Cut large gizzards and livers in half. Place in plastic bag and add sauce. Close bag tightly and turn to coat giblets. Giblets should be prepared just before cooking or refrigerated.

Place a square of wire cloth or fine-mesh cake rack on grill to hold giblets. Or put them in a hinged wire basket for cooking. Grill until crispy; spear hot on wood picks. Liver pieces cook in 3 minutes; hearts, 4 to 5 minutes; and gizzards, 5 to 7 minutes.

CHICKEN LIVER KEBABS

Grilled chicken livers are good any time, but miniature skewers of them make fine hors d'oeuvres with drinks before the main meal.

1½ pounds chicken livers

2 tablespoons oil, plus additional oil for basting

1 tablespoon soy sauce

1 tablespoon dry red wine or chicken broth

¼ teaspoon freshly ground pepper

¼ teaspoon dried or 1 teaspoon minced fresh marjoram

12 pieces scallions, cut in 2-inch lengths

12 mushroom caps

Boiling water

Makes 4 to 6 generous servings.

Pick over chicken livers and discard any discolored ones. Cut large livers in half. Place livers in a bowl. Sprinkle with 2 tablespoons oil, soy sauce, wine or broth, pepper, and marjoram. Mix well, cover, and refrigerate 30 minutes. Blanch vegetables to prevent splitting when threading them on skewers: place scallions and mushrooms in separate bowls, cover with boiling water, and let stand 10 to 15 minutes.

Thread chicken livers, scallion pieces, and mushrooms on skewers, alternating so that meat and vegetable juices will blend while grilling. Brush lightly with oil and grill 4 inches above hot fire, turning and brushing lightly with oil to cook evenly. Livers will require about 10 to 12 minutes to become crispy-coated and pink and tender inside. Avoid overcooking as livers become tough and dry. Serve hot with rice or potatoes.

SPIT–ROASTED CORNISH HENS

Buy the smallest game birds possible, 1¼ pounds, if you can. Four roast-ing on a spit look luxurious. Keep them well-buttered so they don't dry out.

4 Cornish game hens, thawed, if frozen	*Makes 4*
Salt and freshly ground pepper	*large or 8*
Butter, softened	*moderate*
	servings.

Season cavities of birds with salt and pepper. Tie drumsticks to tails and wrap twine around breasts to hold wings in place. Birds can be spitted lengthwise, from neck through body with spit coming out just above tail, or horizontally, diagonally through a wing and thigh on the other side. Fasten spit forks securely. Rub birds heavily with butter.

Push hot coals to back or side in to provide space for drip pan and put pan in place. Engage spit and start motor turning. Roast birds 45 minutes to 1 hour, until thermometer thrust inside thigh joint registers 180 degrees. Brush with more butter while roasting. Remove birds from spit and serve one to a person or split birds and serve half to a person. Pass flavored butter of your choice (pages 204-06).

SPIT–BARBECUED TURKEY

Barbecued turkey was in high fashion when we moved to California in 1960. We arrived at the first four or five dinner parties to which we were invited to find the hosts watching over turkeys turning slowly on spits over charcoal fires. It can be a culinary triumph, juicy and flavorful with sauce. I still prefer the sharp and acidy barbecue sauce that we used on chicken in Florida, but some people like fruity sauces and others like Carolina-style sauces.

1 turkey, 10 to 12 pounds

Barbecue sauce of your choice (pages 190–203)

Makes 10 to 12 servings.

Check clearance between spit and grill and the circumference of turkey before buying it, but a 12-pound bird will turn smoothly on most grills equipped with spits. Brush inside of turkey lightly with barbecue sauce. Run spit from center of neck skin through body and out just above the tail. Fasten tightly with spit forks. Tie wings to turkey with twine and tie legs and tail together below spit rod. Roll spit rod in palms to check the balance.

Place drip pan under spot where spit will turn and push hot coals to back or side. Engage spit, start motor, and grill turkey until skin is blistered and browned. Raise spit so that turkey turns about 7 inches above coals or poke coals to edge, leaving a thin layer to provide moderate heat. Continue grilling and basting turkey. As drippings collect in drip pan, carefully pour into sauce. Grill turkey until internal temperature registers 180 degrees on meat thermometer, 2½ to 3 hours for a 10- to 12-pound turkey. Cut strings and let turkey rest 20 minutes before carving.

GRILLED TURKEY CUTLETS

Years ago, before turkey breast cutlets were generally available in super-markets, we often mystified our friends with these wing-shaped steaks. We would ask Leon, our butcher, to saw cutlets from the breast portion of a hard-frozen turkey. He would put the turkey on the electric meat saw and cut 1/2-inch steaks from just below the wing down to the lower part of the breast. We would save the hind part of the turkey and the wings for other dishes. Now turkey cutlets are in most markets and often are used as a substitute for veal cutlets.

4 to 6 turkey cutlets, 4 ounces each

1 cup oil

1/2 cup dry white wine

2 teaspoons minced fresh or 1/8 teaspoon rubbed sage

Salt and freshly ground pepper

Makes 4 to 6 servings.

Place turkey in a shallow dish and pour oil and wine over it. Sprinkle with sage. Marinate at room temperature 1 hour or in the refrigerator for 3 to 4 hours, turning 2 or 3 times. Bring dish to grill. Remove each turkey cutlet from marinade and let drip into dish.

Place on well-greased grill about 4 inches above hot fire. Grill, turning and basting as needed for even cooking, about 15 minutes, until turkey is done through but not dry. Serve with Lemon Butter (page 204) or a fruit relish or chutney.

TURKEY BREAST VERMILLION

The gentle, easy heat that produces best-tasting meat does not always provide rich color that appeals to many barbecue lovers. This sauce of catsup, brown sugar, and orange juice colors turkey breast well, and slow roasting over a drip pan ensures tender, juicy meat.

2 tablespoons dark brown sugar

1 tablespoon prepared mustard

½ cup orange juice

½ cup catsup

1 turkey breast, bone-in, 6 to 7 pounds

Oil, optional

Makes 6 to 8 servings, with leftovers.

Combine brown sugar, mustard, orange juice, and catsup. Beat together until sugar is dissolved and sauce is mixed. Place turkey in plastic bag, pour in sauce, close bag, and turn to coat turkey. Refrigerate 6 to 8 hours, turning bag every hour or so to coat turkey.

Push hot coals to back or side of firebox and push drip pan in place. Remove turkey, reserving marinade. Place turkey over coals (not drip pan) and brown on all sides. Move turkey over drip pan and baste lightly with marinade. Cover grill or tuck tent of foil around bird to hold in heat. Roast slowly, basting with drippings every 20 to 30 minutes to cook evenly. Allow 2 to 2½ hours. Meat thermometer thrust into meat, not touching bone, will register 175 to 180 degrees when bird is done. Place on hot platter and let rest 20 minutes before carving. Reheat marinade and serve with sliced turkey.

TERIYAKI TURKEY KEBABS

Boned turkey pieces are a wonderful convenience. We prefer thighs for this dish, and they are easy to bone: Just slit them lengthwise and cut the meat off the bone, in case your market doesn't have them.

1 pound boned turkey tenderloins, breast slices,
   or thighs
½ cup soy sauce
2 tablespoons sherry or sake
1 tablespoon sugar
2 teaspoons grated ginger
1 clove garlic, minced
4 bamboo skewers
1 zucchini, cut in 1-inch chunks
1 onion, cut lengthwise in wedges
4 to 8 cherry tomatoes, stems removed

Makes 4 servings.

Cut turkey in cubes. Place in plastic bag. Combine soy sauce, sherry or sake, sugar, ginger, and garlic. Pour over turkey, close bag, and marinate 2 hours in refrigerator. Soak skewers in water 30 minutes. Drain turkey and thread on skewers alternately with zucchini pieces, onion, and tomatoes. Grill over hot fire until browned, then brush with marinade and grill and turn until tender and done, about 15 minutes.

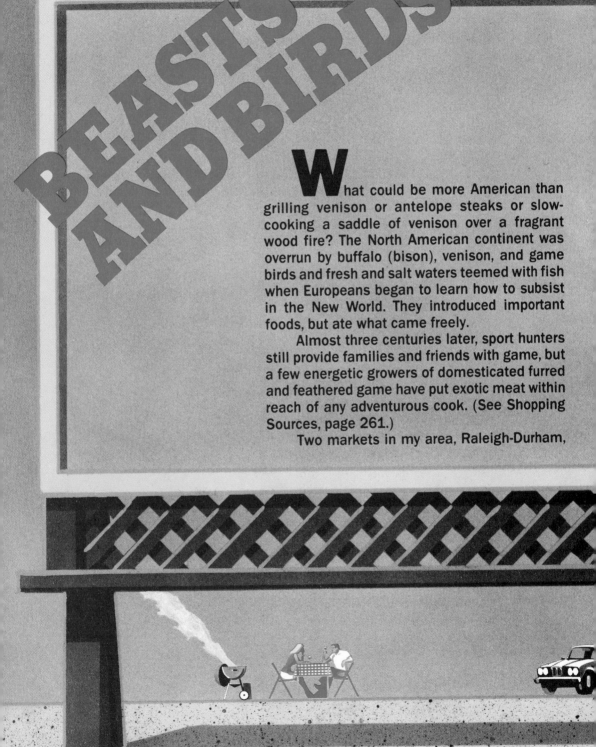

BEASTS AND BIRDS

What could be more American than grilling venison or antelope steaks or slow-cooking a saddle of venison over a fragrant wood fire? The North American continent was overrun by buffalo (bison), venison, and game birds and fresh and salt waters teemed with fish when Europeans began to learn how to subsist in the New World. They introduced important foods, but ate what came freely.

Almost three centuries later, sport hunters still provide families and friends with game, but a few energetic growers of domesticated furred and feathered game have put exotic meat within reach of any adventurous cook. (See Shopping Sources, page 261.)

Two markets in my area, Raleigh-Durham,

North Carolina, offer pheasant or quail any time, and venison or buffalo (bison) on order.

A game dinner off a barbecue grill or smoker s a gastronomic happening, in my view, and we ask only venturesome guests to share it with us. Don't waste venison or bison on finicky eaters!

Game is expensive, so take care in cooking it. In general game is leaner than its conventional counterparts, beef, chicken, turkey, etc., so it needs more fat. Tiny bony birds such as quail should be cooked fast over a hot fire, and for only a few minutes, or they will become dry bones covered with crackles of chewy flesh. Venison or buffalo roasts can be cooked much like Texas brisket, over a low and well-tended fire positioned for indirect heat and with liberal basting. We like an herbed oil and wine marinade and baste for venison rather than the traditional spicy sauce for brisket.

Because game is lean and surface fat usually is trimmed from furred animals, oil or bacon fat is added in a marinade or bacon is laid over the meat before cooking.

A sumptuous meal is no time to worry about cholesterol, but game's leanness makes it top choice for fat control. However, when you add bacon, that's another matter.

WINE–COUNTRY VENISON STEAKS

Marinating venison is customary, but don't overdo it. Long marinating masks the meat's distinctive flavor. Save long-time marinating for roasts.

4 venison steaks, loin or sirloin, 1½ inches thick

½ cup red wine, Zinfandel or Burgundy-type

⅓ cup olive oil

1 clove garlic, minced

2 tablespoons minced parsley

Grape vine trimmings or mesquite chips

Salt and freshly ground black pepper

Makes 4 servings.

Put steaks in bag or shallow dish. Mix together wine, oil, garlic, and parsley. Pour over steaks and turn to coat well. Marinate at room temperature 20 to 30 minutes. Remove meat, reserving marinade. Place steaks over hot fire, and scatter grape trimmings or mesquite that has been soaked in water on fire. Brush steaks with marinade and grill 20 to 25 minutes, best if no more than medium-rare. Turn as needed and brush with marinade while cooking. Season with salt and lots of pepper. Serve on warmed platters.

BARBECUED VENISON WITH JUNIPER

1 loin of venison
1 to 2 cloves garlic, slivered
½ cup red wine, Zinfandel or Burgundy-type
¼ cup oil or vegetable oil
2 teaspoons juniper berries
1 bay leaf, crumbled with rib removed
1 teaspoon whole black pepper
Salt

*Makes 6
servings.*

Cut slits in surface of roast and push in garlic. Place meat in plastic bag. Mix together wine and oil. Pour over meat, seal bag, and marinate in refrigerator 4 to 5 hours. Crush together juniper, bay leaf, and peppers in mortar or between 2 sheets of waxed paper with back of spoon. Drain meat, reserving marinade, and pat dry. Rub seasonings over it. Place drip pan in firebox, pushing fire to front or sides, and place meat over drip pan. Brush with marinade. Close cover or shape tent of foil around venison to hold in heat. Cook and baste periodically with marinade for 3 hours, until thermometer pushed into meaty portion registers 130 (rare) to 155 degrees (well-done). Salt to taste. Let meat stand 20 minutes before carving.

SPIT–BARBECUED VENISON HAUNCH

This is an impressive piece of meat, and a saddle is even more spectacular and more tender. If you order venison, a saddle (double loin attached at the backbone) is as easy to get as haunch, except perhaps at holidays.

1 haunch (leg) of venison, 5 to 6 pounds

2 teaspoons dried mustard

1 tablespoon sugar

1/4 teaspoon freshly ground pepper

1 teaspoon dried thyme leaves

1 teaspoon dried marjoram leaves

1/4 teaspoon ground allspice

1/4 teaspoon ground cloves

1 cup robust red wine, Zinfandel or Burgundy-type

2 tablespoons red wine vinegar

1/4 cup olive oil or as needed

Makes 8 to 10 servings.

Place leg in large plastic bag. In bowl, mix mustard, sugar, pepper, thyme, marjoram, allspice, and cloves well. Stir in wine, then vinegar and oil. Pour over venison. Close bag and marinate in refrigerator 4 to 6 hours or overnight. When fire is ready, push coals to back or sides and put drip pan in place. Remove meat and save marinade. Pat meat dry and place over drip pan on fire. Close grill cover or shape piece of foil around meat to hold in heat. Barbecue 2 hours, until thermometer pushed into meaty portion registers 120 degrees. Add soaked fruitwood or mesquite or hickory chips to coals and smoke 30 minutes longer or until thermometer shows 130 (rare) to 155 degrees (well-done). Let rest on platter 20 to 30 minutes before carving. Cut in very thin slices for maximum tenderness.

BARBECUED RABBIT

Rabbit grills meaty and tender, the firm white meat absorbing any sauce *you baste it with to point up the mild flavor.*

2 fresh-dressed or thawed frozen rabbits, 2½ pounds each

Florida Barbecue Sauce (page 192)

Makes 8 generous servings.

Cut rabbit in halves or quarters. Place meaty side down on grill 5 to 6 inches above hot coals, baste lightly with sauce, and grill until browned, about 10 minutes. Turn and baste lightly. Continue grilling, turning, and basting as needed to cook evenly and prevent charring, about 45 minutes. Make a deep slit into a thigh joint; if juices run clear, rabbit is done. If juice is pink, grill rabbit 10 to 15 minutes longer. Remove rabbit to a warm platter. Serve a quarter to each person, or carve halves in pieces: 2 legs and 2 to 4 body portions per half rabbit. Serve remaining sauce on the side and provide plenty of paper napkins as diners will like to gnaw the bones.

BARBECUED BUFFALO RIBS

Buffalo ranchers like to say that the meat is cooked like beef. This is an exaggeration, as buffalo—the American buffalo (bison) or water buffalo (grown in the South)—is ultra lean and lacks the flavor and tenderness of fine beef. But long slow cooking and a well-sharpened knife to slice it thin make it a novel option to ordinary meats.

1 buffalo rib roast, 6 to 7 pounds
Bone-Broth Basting Sauce (page 195) or Classic
    Soy Marinade (page 200)
Corn or olive oil
Mesquite or hickory chips, dampened

Makes 8 to 12 servings.

Place roast in large plastic bag or bowl, pour sauce over it, close bag, and marinate in refrigerator overnight. Remove meat and reserve marinade. Push hot coals to back or side of firebox and put drip pan in place. Put meat over drip pan, brush with oil, close cover of grill, and cook 3 hours, brushing with marinade and oil every 20 minutes or so. Put chips on fire and continue roasting 1 hour. Test with thermometer. It is rare at 130 degrees, well-done at 155. Buffalo meat is best served rare to medium rare. Let rest 20 minutes before carving. Cut in very thin slices for maximum tenderness.

GRILLED PHEASANT BREASTS

Boned-out breasts marinated and grilled is grand-occasion fare indeed. I serve red cabbage and brown or wild rice in broth made of the pheasant trimmings, as befits splendid food. We use every scrap of pheasants, smoking the legs to serve another time.

2 pheasants, 2½ pounds each, thawed if frozen

4 tablespoons red wine

2 tablespoons olive oil

1 teaspoon *each* dried rosemary and thyme leaves

¼ cup minced parsley or 1½ teaspoons parsley flakes

½ teaspoon salt

¼ teaspoon freshly ground pepper

Additional olive oil

Makes 4 servings.

Bone pheasant breasts (page 135), leaving upper wing parts intact. Reserve bones and trimmings for broth, fat for cooking red cabbage, and legs to smoke. Combine wine, olive oil, and seasonings in measuring cup. Mix well. Place pheasant breasts in plastic bag, add marinade, seal bag, and turn to coat meat with marinade. Place in bowl and refrigerate 3 hours or longer.

Pour marinade into bowl. With tongs, remove pheasant breasts and place on grill over hot coals. Fire should be medium-size, as large fire will scorch birds before they are done. Brush birds lightly with marinade. Cover grill and cook 45 minutes, or until pheasant is browned and juices run clear when bird is pierced with a fork. Turn and baste birds every 15 minutes. When marinade is exhausted, baste with additional olive oil. Serve hot with Old World Red Cabbage (page 235), Wild or Brown Rice in Pheasant Broth (page 236), and cranberry sauce or chutney.

TO REMOVE AND BONE PHEASANT BREASTS

Place pheasant back side down on board. With sharp knife, cut joints, leaving top section of wing attached. Pull away visible fat in body and at cavity openings to use for cooking red cabbage. On each side of bird, locate hip joint with tip of knife and sever cleanly, cutting away from body at joint. Set aside legs and wing tips.

Remove breast from back by cutting from shoulder joint along curved rib line to bottom of body. Open flat onto board and cut shoulder joint to remove back from breast.

Turn breast cavity side up, slit membrane that covers breast bone, and scrape flesh away from bone. When breast bone is freed, smack sharply with heel of hand and remove breast bone. Cut breast lengthwise in two portions, each containing a wing and half the meat.

With knife angled toward bone and fingers, work rib cage and shoulder and collar (wishbone) bones free and pull out. Cut back in two portions, with section containing "oyster" reserved for smoking and the other for stockpot.

Marinate and grill breasts. Refrigerate trimmings and other parts, then marinate legs and meaty backs and smoke.

PORT–WINE DUCK

Domestic ducks are not as fat as they once were and farm-raised wild ducks are generally lean, so both lend themselves to barbecuing.

2 ducks

Makes 4 servings.

¼ cup red port wine

1 tablespoon balsamic vinegar

¼ cup finely chopped celery leaves

¼ cup olive oil

1 clove garlic, minced

½ teaspoon cracked black pepper

2 onions quartered and studded with 4 whole cloves each

½ green bell pepper, quartered

1 apple or orange, quartered

More olive oil, optional

Place ducks in plastic bag. Combine port, vinegar, celery, ¼ cup oil, garlic, and pepper. Pour over ducks, close bags, and marinate in refrigerator 1 to 3 hours. Drain ducks and put onion, bell pepper, and apple or orange in cavities. Push hot coals to back or side of grill and put drip pan in place. Put ducks over drip pan, close cover, and grill 1½ hours or until thermometer registers 175 degrees. Wild duck should be brushed with oil every 15 minutes to keep it moist and if domestic duck appears dry, brush with oil. Remove ducks to warm platter and let rest 20 minutes before carving. Cut into quarters to serve, allowing a breast and leg half for each person. Serve with wild rice or bread stuffing cooked separately.

SPATCHCOCKED QUAIL ON SKEWERS

*T*his *method of cutting and cooking quail can be adapted to small Cornish hens — almost as lean as quail, and good marinated and cooked quickly.*

4 to 8 quail

½ cup olive oil

¼ cup dry white wine

¼ cup chicken or quail broth

2 tablespoons white wine vinegar

2 tablespoons minced celery leaves

1 teaspoon coarsely ground pepper

Grape vine trimmings or hickory chips

Salt to taste

Makes 1 or 2 birds per person, for 4 to 8 servings.

Remove giblets from birds and reserve for broth or other uses. To spatchcock birds, cut off wing tips between top and second joint of wings, using poultry shears or sharp knife. Cut close to backbone and remove it. Open the bird out and cut wishbone in half and pull it out. With cavity side up, smack breast bone with heel of hand to break it and flatten bird. Make a small cut in each side of skin between leg and breastbone and tuck in knee joint. Thread birds onto two sturdy skewers passed through wings, then thigh joints. Two birds may be skewered together but allow space between them. Repeat with all birds.

Place skewered birds in shallow dish. Beat together oil, wine, broth, vinegar, celery leaves, and pepper. Brush over birds, turn, and brush on other side. Let stand at room temperature 30 minutes. Drain any marinade and juices into cup. Add grape cuttings or dampened hickory chips to hot fire. Place birds skin side up on grill over hot fire. Grill until browned, turn, brush with marinade, and grill on other side until browned. Grill, baste, and turn until crispy on the outside and juicy on the inside, a total of 12 to 15 minutes.

SMOKY GINGER DUCKLING

Generally, I don't precook meat before barbecuing it, but this method rids duck of some of the excessive fat. The elegant dish is worth it and you avoid dangerous flare-ups and messy clean-up.

1 duckling, 4 to 5 pounds

2 or 3 thin slices fresh ginger root, cut in fine shreds,
    plus additional sliced ginger for garnish

2 tablespoons duck drippings

2 cloves garlic, minced

½ cup orange juice

Roasted Orange Halves (page 247)

Makes 4 small or 2 large servings.

I prefer fresh duckling, but if using frozen thaw it thoroughly in refrigerator. Clip off wing tips, remove neck and giblets, and freeze for other uses. Preheat oven to 400 degrees. Place duckling breast side up in a shallow pan on rack and roast 1 hour. Puncture skin with fork in several places to allow fat to cook out, turn duckling back side up, and roast 30 minutes longer or until juices in cavity lose their red color. Cool duckling until it can be handled. With poultry or kitchen shears cut out backbone. Cut duckling in half along breastbone. Working with small knife and fingers, pull rib cages from each half of duck. Sprinkle cavities with shredded ginger. In a small saucepan heat the 2 tablespoons duck drippings, add garlic, and cook until golden. Stir in orange juice and heat slightly.

Place duckling halves skin side down over drip pan surrounded by hot coals or with hot coals at back. Turn and baste duckling with sauce. Close grill cover or tuck a loose tent of foil around duck to hold in heat. Grill 45 minutes or until meat is juicy, skin browned and crispy, and duck done. Remove to platter and garnish with more ginger and Roasted Orange Halves.

FISH AND SEAFOOD

Barbecuing fish is a great American tradition. Indians grilled salmon over alderwood fires on Puget Sound long before Europeans arrived. On beaches near Cape Hatteras in the fall when mullet is fat, Indians would spear the fish on green sticks and roast it over campfires. In Florida, I've seen Seminoles roast whole fish at the edge of a campfire. Some historians believe that early settlers in Savannah learned to roast oysters from Indians, but in any case diaries of settlers record oyster roasts as social diversion only a few months after the first colonists came in 1733.

Yet it took us some years to adopt fish as regular fare for the grill. No fish tastes so good as one caught, cleaned, and cooked on the spot, and we were doing this when we fished the lakes and canals of Florida. Generally the cooking on fishing trips was rather plain, the cleaned fish   seasoned lightly with salt, pepper, and lime juice and cooked over a hot fire eight to ten minutes, plenty of time for panfish and fillets.

This summer we went all out, cooking fish two or three times a week. The turning point came when we discovered a remedy for the constant hazard of fish sticking to the grill. That evening, I wrapped fish fillets in cabbage leaves to hold in a bit of marinade and keep the fish moist. The cabbage was cooked to a crisp and we discarded it. But wonder of wonders, the fish did not stick and came out moist and delicious.

Fish is naturally tender and needs only enough cooking to set the juices. Pierce the fish near the center with the tip of a knife after about six minutes. When it is done, the flesh looks translucent, almost opaque, not flaky.

The recipes in this section are more elaborate than fishing trip cookery but reflect my feeling that fine fish needs little embellishment. Smoke and outdoors is enough. I like mild woods for smoking fish— hickory, fruit wood, or, in Florida, Australian pine added to the fire just before the fish is finished. Mesquite is too powerful, for my taste.

Catch your own fish and take care of it before cooking or buy the very finest fish you can get. Top-quality, well-handled fish is juicy, tender, and charmingly "fishy" when the marinade is designed to accent but not overwhelm the pure clean flavor of fish, and the fire is built hot but not too pungent.

SWORDFISH BARBECUED IN CABBAGE LEAVES

Mako shark steaks are a good alternative to swordfish, and usually less expensive. We introduced many people who haven't had the courage to try shark to this great fish for the grill. Thick, fresh tuna steaks work well, too.

4 swordfish or mako shark steaks, 1 inch thick

¼ cup rice wine vinegar

2 teaspoons soy sauce

1 teaspoon sugar

1 tablespoon sherry or sake (Japanese rice wine)

2 teaspoons minced or grated ginger root

¼ cup (2 small) finely sliced green onion or
     scallion with tops

1 tablespoon corn or vegetable oil

4 large cabbage leaves, blanched 1 minute in boiling water

Makes 4 servings.

Place fish in plastic bag or shallow dish. In bowl, mix together vinegar, soy sauce, sugar, sherry or sake, ginger root, and green onion or scallion. Blend well and stir in oil. Pour over fish. Close bag and marinate 30 minutes at room temperature or 3 to 4 hours in refrigerator. Drain fish, reserving marinade.

Place cabbage leaves cupped side up on grill over hot coals and place a fish steak on each. Gently tuck leaves around fish, leaving openings for circulation of smoke. Close grill or place a loose tent of foil over fish to hold in heat. Grill 3 to 4 minutes, unwrap, brush fish with reserved marinade, turn, and grill 5 to 6 minutes longer, until fish is translucent near center when pierced with fork or tip of a knife.

Meanwhile, heat remaining marinade. Arrange fish on warm platter, discarding cabbage, and pour sauce over it or serve sauce on side.

NONSTICK STRATEGY

Sticking to the grill is the bane of barbecue cooks who want to cook fish. There are several ways to prevent it, some described in individual recipes.

Our newest trick is to loosely wrap fish fillets, steaks, or individual servings of shrimp or shelled seafood in cabbage or lettuce leaves. The greens are wilted, but the fish comes off the grill easily. Well-oiled aluminum foil pricked with holes to allow heat circulation works as well.

Oiling the grill or spritzing it with nonstick cooking spray helps. Some chefs spritz the fish itself, which is okay, though the flavor of the spray is not appealing.

Putting fish in a hinged wire basket that is well oiled lets you turn it without having to scrape it off the grill where it sticks. Generally fish can be lifted gently from the wire basket.

A salmon or other fish fillet with skin need be cooked only meaty side up. When the fish is taken up, only bits of skin cling to the pregreased grill.

BARBECUED FISH WITH FENNEL

Fennel softens the flavor of robust-flavored fish such as mackerel and enhances delicate fish such as sea bass. Thick slices of fennel also help prevent fish from sticking to the grill. Salmon, cod, and flounder are good choices for this recipe, too.

1 whole fish, cleaned and head cut off, 3 to 7 pounds

1 large head fennel, 1½ to 2 pounds

Juice of 1 lemon

Melted butter

Lemon wedges

Makes 6 to 12 servings.

Leave skin on fish and have it split almost through and the long backbone removed. Slice fennel lengthwise, including outside stalks, as they will go on the grill.

Fill fish with tender inside slices of fennel. Skewer fish closed over fennel and tie, if necessary. Grease grill thoroughly with oil or melted butter.

When fire is hot, place outer fennel slices on grill to serve as a bed for fish. Place fish on fennel on grill, sprinkle with lemon juice, and brush generously with butter. (Or fish and fennel can be placed in hinged wire grill.) Cover grill or shape a loose tent of foil over fish. Grill 15 minutes. Brush with butter and turn fish. Continue cooking, turning, and basting with butter to cook evenly until fish is opaque near center when pierced with a fork, about 40 minutes for a 3-pound fish, up to 1 hour for a 7-pound fish. Place fish on warm platter, carefully lifting from grill with broad spatula and fork or spoon. Discard scorched fennel tops. Fresh fennel can be added as garnish. Pull skin off top of fish with fingers, loosening it with a fork. Garnish with lemon wedges and serve with more melted butter.

BARBECUED WHOLE FISH

A *whole fish makes a splendid display, set on its platter with parsley or watercress and lemon wedges.*

1 firm-fleshed white-meated fish (red snapper, Pacific
    rock cod, or sea bass), cleaned with head left on,
    2½ pounds
Salt and freshly ground pepper
½ cup oil
Fresh thyme, rosemary, or dill
2 tablespoons lemon juice
1 stick (½ cup) melted butter or Anchovy or Sage
    Butter (pages 204–05)

Makes
4 to 6
servings.

Sprinkle fish lightly with salt and pepper. Beat together oil, 2 tablespoons minced herb, and lemon juice. Liberally brush inside and outside of fish. Rub grill heavily with oil.

Place fish in hinged wire grill or put it directly on the barbecue grill 5 to 6 inches above hot coals and close cover or shape a loose tent of foil over fish to hold in heat. Grill about 7 minutes, until lightly browned. Brush again with oil mixture, carefully turn fish, using 2 spatulas, close grill, and cook fish 7 to 8 minutes longer or until fish flakes with a fork. Just before fish is done add fresh herb sprigs to fire for added aroma. Remove fish carefully to platter and brush with remaining oil mixture. Serve with melted butter or Anchovy or Sage butter sauce.

WHOLE SALMON IN FOIL

A cradle of foil facilitates turning fish on a grill and prevents sticking. A fish-shaped rack works as well, but finding the rack large enough for a fish I want to cook this way is difficult. The foil is left open to allow smoky aroma to penetrate.

Oil or butter

1 whole salmon, 2½ to 3 pounds

Salt and freshly ground pepper

Juice of 1 lemon

1 tablespoon olive or corn oil

3 to 4 sprigs fresh dill, plus ¼ cup chopped

1 teaspoon Dijon-style mustard

½ stick (¼ cup) butter, softened

Lemon wedges

Makes 6 servings.

Tear off a sheet of heavy-duty foil long enough to cradle fish, leaving an end piece for turning up. Poke holes at intervals in foil, using a pencil or ice pick, to allow smoke to circulate. Grease foil heavily with oil or butter. Place fish on foil. Season cavity with salt, pepper, lemon juice, and 1 tablespoon oil. Place dill sprigs in cavity and let stand at room temperature 20 minutes. Turn foil up around fish to form a boat.

Place fish in foil on grill over hot coals. Grill 5 minutes, then with wide spatula and tongs carefully turn fish in foil. Grill 5 minutes and turn again. Continue grilling and turning to cook evenly, until fish is opaque when tested with fork near center. Allow 25 to 30 minutes total cooking time for salmon.

Meanwhile, beat together chopped dill, mustard, and butter. Carefully lift foil off grill and roll fish onto warm platter. Garnish with lemon wedges and serve dill-butter sauce on the side.

WHICH SPECIES?

Firm-fleshed, meaty fish are logical for barbecuing. A favorite is swordfish, cut in steaks. Mako shark is a sturdy fish for the grill, too. Most whole fish works well on the grill. The skin helps prevent crumbling and overcooking. Try whole red snapper, sea bass, redfish, mackerel or kingfish, cobia, or grouper cut in steaks or fillets. Thick codfish fillets work, too.

Whole fish is juicier and easier to handle on the grill if the head is left on. The head can be lopped off before serving the fish to squeamish diners, but a garnished whole fish, head and all, is dramatic food indeed.

Salmon—fillets, steaks, or whole small fish—are perfect for grilling. With skin on, they are easy. Farm-raised salmon from Norway is available year round, but you should wait for North American fresh salmon in summer from the North Atlantic, late summer for Pacific salmon. Wild salmon has a short season, but is worth the wait.

Softer fish, mullet, catfish, and flatfish such as flounder, sole, and halibut, or thin fillets of almost any fish are hard to manage, but dexterous chefs who master them find that their taste is tops. Bluefish and mackerel are also good.

FISH GRILLED OVER
VINE CUTTINGS

We *first had fish grilled this way at Château Canon in St.-Émilion one April when driving through Bordeaux. Wine grapevines are pruned each autumn and the cuttings are dried and saved for burning. As we drove into the broad graveled parking space at the entry of the château, a rosy-cheeked girl was tending the fish as it grilled over a tiny fire set in a garage, since a light rain was falling.*

1 sea bass, cleaned, about 3 pounds *Makes*
Salt and freshly ground pepper *6 to 8*
2 or 3 sprigs fresh tarragon *servings.*
Melted butter
Vine cuttings or other small sweet wood twigs
Lemon wedges and parsley

A fish-shaped basket with short legs is ideal for grilling fish over dried vine cuttings. If you don't have a fish grill, build the fire in a small barbecue grill. Season fish cavity and skin with salt and pepper. Place tarragon sprigs in cavity and skewer fish closed. Place in basket. Brush generously with butter. Choose a smooth stone or level ground (the cement floor of an open carriage house held the fish grill that we observed in Bordeaux) for the fish grill. Vine cuttings burn fast, so have plenty of them to replenish fire as needed.

Lay the fire in an oval a little longer than the fish grill, ignite it, and when very hot place fish grill slightly to the leeward side of the fire. Grill the fish, flipping the basket to turn the fish as it browns and cooks and basting with more butter. Feed the fire as needed to keep it hot. Fish is done when it is opaque when tested with a fork. This will take about 20 minutes if fish is turned carefully and fire is kept burning furiously. Place fish on platter and garnish with lemon wedges and parsley. Serve with more melted butter.

BARBECUED CATCH OF THE DAY

Every fisherman's tackle box should contain a jar of the butter with oil and another jar of citrus juice or the fresh fruit, salt, pepper, and a lemon for this fine fare.

4 schoolboy snappers, bluefish, walleyed pike,
   rockfish, sunfish, or brook trout, ½ to
   1 pound each
½ stick (¼ cup) butter
¼ cup vegetable or olive oil
2 tablespoons lemon or orange juice
Salt and freshly ground pepper
Lemon wedges

Makes 4 servings.

Have fish cleaned; fish is juicier if cooked with the head on, but cut it off if you insist. Thoroughly grease a hinged wire grill. Arrange fish, not quite touching, in grill. Close and fasten grill.

Place over hot coals. In small saucepan, heat butter and oil. Stir in citrus juice and brush generously on fish. Grill until browned, turn, and baste. Cook 15 to 20 minutes, just until fish looks opaque when tested with a fork. Season with salt and pepper, then remove fish carefully to platter. Serve with lemon wedges.

FISH FILLETS IN ORANGE SAUCE

Californians marinate fish this way before barbecuing it, and you'll find similar seasonings for fish in Spain and northern Africa.

2 pounds fish fillets (snapper, cod, sea bass, monkfish)
¾ cup orange juice
1 teaspoon grated orange peel
¼ cup each oil and dry vermouth
½ teaspoon salt
Freshly ground pepper to taste
2 cloves garlic, minced
Lemon wedges

Makes 4 to 6 servings.

Place fish in a shallow dish. Combine orange juice and peel, oil, vermouth, salt, pepper, and garlic. Pour over fish and marinate 30 minutes at room temperature. Drain fish and place in a well-greased hinged wire grill or grease barbecue grill liberally.

Grill fish 3 to 4 inches above hot coals 12 to 15 minutes, just until fish flakes when tested with a fork. Remove fish to platter and garnish with lemon wedges. Serve tartar sauce, too, if desired.

FISH AND SEAFOOD

GRILLED FISH WITH GINGER–SOY SAUCE

Ginger perks up almost any fish but is especially good on salmon. Peel the root and grate it or put it through a garlic press.

¼ cup *each* sweet sherry and soy sauce

1 tablespoon grated or minced ginger root

1 large clove garlic, minced

2 fillets salmon (tail piece) or sea bass,
    1½ pounds each

Peanut or vegetable oil

Makes 4 to 6 servings.

Combine sherry, soy sauce, ginger, and garlic. Mix well. Pour over fish in plastic bag or shallow dish. Turn fish in sauce or turn bag to coat fish well. Marinate at room temperature 30 minutes or in refrigerator for 3 hours or longer, turning 2 or 3 times. Remove fish from marinade and pour marinade into small saucepan. Brush fish well with oil, place in wire grill that has been well oiled, and fasten shut.

Grill over hot coals, basting with marinade and turning now and then. Grill until fish is opaque when pierced near center with fork. Remove to platter and serve with remaining hot marinade.

CHARCOAL–GRILLED HALIBUT AND OTHER FISH STEAKS

Thin fish steaks dry out and are difficult to turn on the grill. We have them cut 1 to 1½ inches thick.

4 to 6 halibut, grouper, or codfish steaks, 1 inch thick
¼ cup lemon juice
½ cup corn or olive oil
Salt and freshly ground pepper
¼ cup minced parsley or 1 tablespoon minced fresh
    tarragon
1 tablespoon minced onion
Lemon wedges

Makes 4 to 6 servings.

Place fish in shallow dish or plastic bag. Combine lemon juice with oil, salt and pepper to taste, parsley or tarragon, and onion. Pour over fish. Cover and marinate at room temperature 30 minutes. Place fish in hinged wire grill to facilitate turning or place on cabbage or lettuce leaves on greased grill.

Grill over hot coals 5 to 6 minutes on each side, until fish is opaque when tested with a fork near centers of steaks. Serve with lemon garnish.

FROZEN OR FRESH!

Purists refuse to believe that frozen fish can be grilled or barbecued. These folks generally, by virtue of their locations (next to a fresh-fish port or well-stocked fish department in a supermarket) or professions (a chef, in daily contact with prime dealers), can have fresh fish at any time.

Until recently, we bought in a market that offered frozen fish or stale, so-called fresh fish that had been trucked two or three days after it was unloaded from a slow boat from the fishing grounds. Often the frozen was better.

Now we live in a spot where really fresh shrimp is available. A few one-night shrimp boats land at the fishing port only 100 miles away. From the same port our fish store brings in fresh grouper, mullet, snapper, and sea bass. These are first choice for us.

But if stale, overaged fish trucked hundreds of miles or frozen fish are the options, we prefer frozen.

To use frozen fish, partially thaw it. Individually frozen cod fillets, for example, need only 20 to 30 minutes on the kitchen counter before going on the grill. Brush it with marinade, set it on a cabbage or lettuce leaf to discourage sticking, and grill it until opaque.

FISH ROASTED IN TI LEAVES

Mahimahi (dolphin fish) is classic for this Hawaiian-inspired roast. Ti leaves can be purchased from a florist who specializes in tropical flowers. I like banana leaves (from a florist, too, if you don't have a banana herb growing in your patio). Corn husks are good in summer and, in a pinch, aluminum foil works.

1½ pounds fish fillets or a 2½-pound whole fish, cleaned (mahimahi, monkfish chunks, snapper, halibut, rock cod)
About 4 to 6 large ti leaves
Sea salt or ice cream salt
2 or 3 slices bacon, chopped
1 small onion, diced fine
1 bay leaf, crumbled, rib removed

Makes 4 to 6 servings.

Rub fish on all sides with salt. Place on leaves, overlapping them to form a leakproof package. Sprinkle with bacon, onion, and bay leaf. Wrap leaves around fish and tie with stem of ti leaf or kitchen twine.

Grill over hot coals, turning to cook evenly, until fish is opaque when tested with a fork, 30 to 45 minutes for whole fish or chunks, 15 to 20 minutes for fillets. Arrange fresh leaves on platter, place fish on leaves, and trim away wilted leaves.

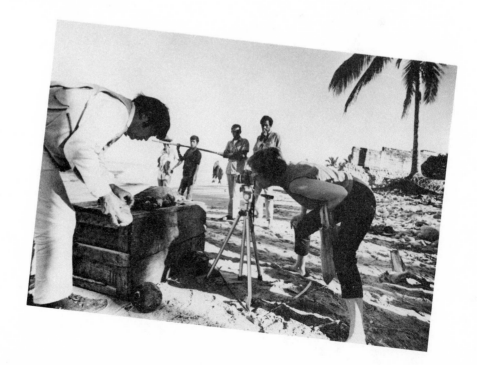

FISH AND SEAFOOD

GRILLED SPANISH MACKEREL FILLETS

Steve Trumbull, *who considered fishing holes part of his beat at the Miami* **Herald,** *cooked mackerel this way. Jane, his wife, made the most fabulous tartar sauce you'll ever taste.*

4 fresh-caught Spanish mackerel, about 1½ pounds each
Juice of 1 or 2 limes
Salt, freshly ground pepper, and dill weed
Oil
Jane Trumbull's Tartar Sauce (page 206)
Lime wedges

Makes 4 servings.

Have fish cleaned and filleted. (Doing this at the dock saves a lot of muss at home.) Wrap fillets in plastic wrap or tightly in waxed paper and keep very cold until an hour before cooking. Spread fillets flesh side up on a sheet of waxed paper. Sprinkle generously with lime juice, cutting another lime if needed. Sprinkle lightly with salt, pepper, and dill weed. Oil grill thoroughly or place fish in a well-oiled hinged grill.

Grill fish skin side down over hot coals until skin is blistered and browned. Brush with oil, turn, and grill 7 to 10 minutes, until fish is opaque when tested with a fork. Serve hot with tartar sauce and lime wedges.

TURKISH–STYLE SWORDFISH KEBABS

2 swordfish or mako shark steaks, 1 inch thick, about
    2 pounds total

½ teaspoon paprika

2 tablespoons olive oil

1 tablespoon grated onion

10 to 12 bay leaves

Juice of 1 lemon

1 tablespoon finely chopped fresh parsley, preferably
    flat-leaf

½ teaspoon salt

Lemon wedges

Makes 6 servings.

Cut swordfish or mako shark in 1-inch cubes, discarding skin and bone. In a plastic bag or bowl combine fish, paprika, 1 tablespoon oil, onion, and bay leaves. Cover tightly and refrigerate 2 to 3 hours. Thread fish on skewers, spearing a bay leaf between fish cubes at intervals.

Grill over hot fire, turning to cook evenly, until fish is cooked through but not dry, about 12 minutes. Meanwhile, beat together remaining tablespoon oil, lemon juice, parsley, and salt. Push fish off skewers onto platter and discard bay leaves. Garnish with lemon wedges and serve with sauce.

SAVANNAH OYSTER ROAST

If you're a guest in this city that celebrates its culinary heritage, Fernandina Beach in north Florida, or Cumberland Island, on the state line, in the late winter, you're sure to be invited to an oyster roast. You may be transported to the scene of the roast by boat along creeks and rivers lined with cypress trees, draped with Spanish moss and camellias in bloom.

Oysters in the shell, at least 12 per person
Salt and freshly ground pepper
Melted butter
Lemon or lime wedges
Hot pepper and Worcestershire sauces

Scrub oysters to eliminate any mud on shells. For easier handling, cover grill with heavy-duty foil with holes poked in it or a sheet of metal (professionals use sheet metal and rake oysters on it while cooking), or oysters can be roasted directly on the grill.

Place oysters over hot coals. Cover grill or shape loose tent of foil over oysters to hold in heat. When shells open, in about 6 minutes, oysters are done. Arrange on plates, deep halves of shells down, and serve hot. Cut the muscles from shells so eaters can remove oysters, or provide small sharp knives at tables.

Each person seasons oysters to taste with salt and pepper, then dips them in butter with lemon or lime juice and hot pepper and/or Worcestershire sauce. Continue cooking oysters until nobody wants more. The classic accompaniments to oysters are French fries or potato chips in this age of casual dining. Early settlers roasted oysters to precede a major dinner or lunch.

OYSTER ROAST

"This is one of the most fashionable of our winter sports, and every stranger must needs be entertained in this alfresco manner during the season.

"Most of the country homes at the nearby watering places have great tables in the yards, and a deep trough where the oysters may be roasted over the open fire.

"Each guest is furnished with a little bowl of melted butter, seasoned to taste with lemon or Worcestershire Sauce, and armed with a fork. As the oysters are roasted they are opened by the colored men—or by the guests themselves if they be so accomplished—dipped hot into the waiting sauce, and eaten *ad infinitum*. It is incredible how many you can eat, and just when you have decided to stop from sheer exhaustion, a great dish of Hopping John, accompanied by a salad and hot biscuits is passed, and you cannot resist this noble combination. The oysters, *au naturel,* you find have been but an hors d'oeuvre to the grand repast, which is brought to a close with cups of steaming coffee." From *The Savannah Cook Book* by Harriet Ross Colquitt, Colonial Publishers, Charleston.

CLAMS STEAMED IN FOIL

This way of steaming clams provides clambakelike results without having to dig a hole in the sand. If the grill is large enough, put fresh corn on it to butter and eat with the clams.

3 dozen littleneck clams

1 small onion, minced

1 stick (½ cup) butter

2 tablespoons minced parsley

2 cloves garlic, minced

2 tablespoons lemon juice

Freshly ground pepper to taste

Makes 6 servings.

Scrub clams thoroughly with a stiff brush and discard any clams with cracked or open shells. Tear off 6 large squares of heavy-duty aluminum foil and place 6 clams in center of each. Sprinkle with onion. Melt butter and stir in parsley, garlic, lemon juice, and pepper. Pour over clams. Fold foil packets tightly closed at top.

Grill over hot coals 7 to 10 minutes, shaking packets and changing positions from outer edges to center to cook clams evenly. Clams open when done. Place each packet in large soup bowl and let diners open their own. Provide spoons for broth and forks for clams.

GRILLED LOBSTER TAILS

One summer, sailing from Miami to the Bahamas, we anchored in a sheltered cove on a stormy evening. Within a minute a smack boat, the favorite Bahamian fishing boat at that time, appeared as if from nowhere. The fishermen wanted to barter freshly caught rock lobster for cigarettes. We negotiated a trade, to our great delight, and grilled the tails over a brazier set in the dinghy. One of the cardinal rules of carefree sailing is fire prevention. Thus our charcoal fire was set in the dinghy so it could be cut loose in case it should get out of control, though in years of sailing we never had a mishap. Grilled lobster tails make an impressive back yard barbecue for guests, and I had lobster tails grilled over a fire seasoned with mesquite chips in a restaurant on Mission Bay in San Diego only a few days before setting down this method of cooking that we have enjoyed for years.

1 or 2 lobster tails, about 7 ounces each, per person

Butter or oil

Lemon or lime wedges

Salt and freshly ground pepper

Melted butter or Anchovy or Green Butter
     (pages 204 and 206)

Thaw lobster tails, if frozen. For a "piggyback lobster tail," cut the shell down the back lengthwise, using poultry shears or kitchen shears and leaving tail fan intact. Do not remove undershell. With fingers, pull lobster meat through the slit. Brush heavily with butter or oil and sprinkle lightly with lemon or lime juice. Grill meat side down over hot coals until meat is opaque but still tender, about 7 minutes. Serve hot with melted butter or Anchovy or Green Butter Sauce.

For a "fan-cut lobster tail," snip away undershell and small legs, using shears. Snap tail back hard to break it and release the shell ligaments that tighten while cooking. Or spear the tail end to end with a skewer to keep it from curling while cooking. Spread heavily with butter or oil and sprinkle with lemon or lime juice. Grill shell side down over hot coals about 4 minutes, until shell is brown. Brush again with oil or butter, turn flesh side down, and grill 3 minutes or until meat is opaque but still tender. Serve with melted butter or Anchovy or Green Butter Sauce.

GRILLED CLAMS OREGANATE

24 clams in the shell

3 large cloves garlic, minced

1/4 cup minced fresh or 1 tablespoon dried oregano

2 tablespoons minced parsley

1 cup fine dry bread crumbs

2 tablespoons oil

Makes 6 appetizer servings or 2 main-dish servings.

Scrub clams thoroughly and discard any that are not live. Hardshells close their shells when tapped if they are live, siphon clams constrict their necks.

Place clams on grill over hot coals. In a small skillet combine garlic, oregano, parsley, bread crumbs, and oil. Stir together to form a crumbly mixture and heat at the edge of the grill while clams are roasting. When clam shells open (after about 5 minutes), lift off top shells using mitts to protect your hands. Drop a spoonful of the herbed crumbs on each clam and heat a minute or 2. Serve at once.

GRILLED SHRIMP WITH BACON

Buy *the largest shrimp you can find for this dish, as peeling tiny shrimp is a chore and tiny shrimp cook dry before you know it.*

2 pounds jumbo shrimp
1/2 teaspoon salt
1/4 cup lemon juice
1/4 cup catsup
3 dashes hot pepper sauce
1 clove garlic, crushed
1/2 cup oil
1/2 pound sliced bacon
Lemon wedges

Makes
4 to 6
servings.

Shell and clean uncooked shrimp. In a bowl mix salt, lemon juice, catsup, pepper sauce, garlic, and oil. Marinate shrimp in mixture 30 minutes at room temperature. Cut each bacon slice crosswise into 4 or 5 pieces. Remove shrimp from marinade, reserving the sauce. Thread shrimp and bacon pieces alternately on skewers, leaving space between to allow heat to penetrate.

Grill over hot coals just until shrimp is opaque and bacon is crisp, 8 to 10 minutes. Turn several times while grilling to cook evenly and brush each time with the reserved sauce. Bacon drippings make fire flare up, so keep a water spritzer handy. Serve shrimp at once with lemon wedges.

GRILLED SCALLOPS IN BACON

Guests eat as many of these as you can cook when passed as appetizers, and they are great for a quickly improvised dinner.

2 pounds sea scallops
2 tablespoons oil
2 tablespoons lemon juice
1/4 teaspoon white pepper
About 1/2 pound sliced bacon
Lemon wedges

Makes 6 to 8 main-dish servings.

In a bowl combine scallops with oil, lemon juice, and pepper. Mix well, cover, and marinate at room temperature 30 minutes, turning once or twice. Cut bacon slices lengthwise in half, then crosswise, making 4 pieces of each slice of bacon. You will need a piece for each scallop. Remove scallops from marinade and wrap each in a piece of bacon. Spear with a wood pick soaked in water to prevent charring or thread 3 or 4 bacon-wrapped scallops on each short skewer, allowing space between for heat penetration. Scallops on short picks are more easily turned if placed in a hinged wire grill.

Grill over hot coals for 5 to 7 minutes, turning as needed to cook evenly and prevent flare-ups. Serve at once with lemon wedges.

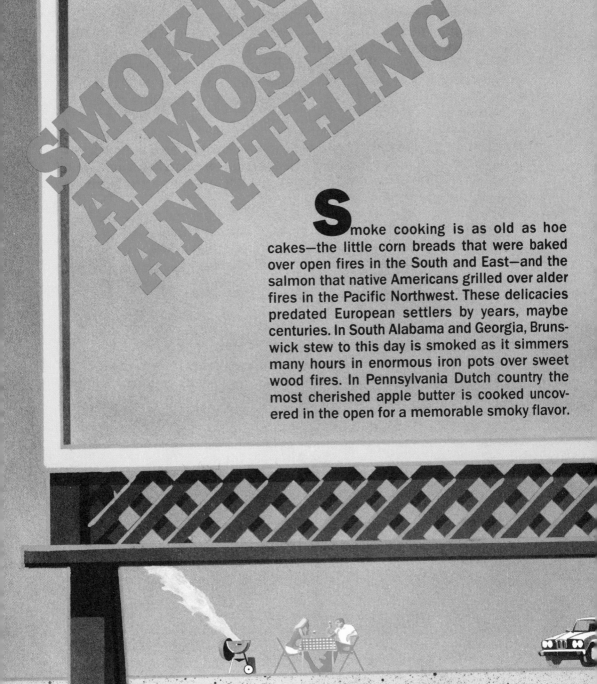

SMOKING ALMOST ANYTHING

Smoke cooking is as old as hoe cakes—the little corn breads that were baked over open fires in the South and East—and the salmon that native Americans grilled over alder fires in the Pacific Northwest. These delicacies predated European settlers by years, maybe centuries. In South Alabama and Georgia, Brunswick stew to this day is smoked as it simmers many hours in enormous iron pots over sweet wood fires. In Pennsylvania Dutch country the most cherished apple butter is cooked uncovered in the open for a memorable smoky flavor.

I used to have a small galvanized metal smoker-oven with a low-power electrical heat unit and tray to hold the smoking medium—dampened chips. We smoked turkeys, hung from a hook in the top of it, fish, and pork chops once in a while. But the glamour faded. Too much smoked turkey and pheasant was available by mail order, and self-service meat counters were full of smoked pork chops. So, in a move, I left the little smoker to a thrift shop.

A few years later, smoked food had come back in fashion. Salads of smoked poultry and meats were everywhere. Friends landmarked drives along beach roads where there were places for smoked mullet, shrimp, and other seafood. These new smoked foods brought to mind the joys of smoke cooking.

So recently we bought a water smoker. It is larger and does more than the simple box smoker of years past. A waist-high black metal drum contains four levels. At the bottom is a fire pan, just over it a water pan, and above that two racks. Each rack accommodates two or three whole chickens, a pork butt, several pounds of spareribs, or six to eight pounds of fish fillets. The heat is gentle, which softens fibers in less expensive cuts of meat, so the time required is three or four times as long as that of conventional barbecue or kitchen cooking.

The first weekend we had it we smoked ten pounds of pork ribs and a few fillets of fresh Pacific salmon. We enjoyed every minute of peering into the smoker, smelling the smoke as it rose through trees shading the deck, and watching the ruddy color of pork as it smoked. By dinnertime, Frank and I smelled like firebugs, rather tasty firebugs from mesquite

chips. (To be honest, you need not hang around, and lifting the lid to peek is a no-no—it lets the heat escape. We were playing with a new toy!)

But the triumph was in the tasting. We feasted, our guests loved the food, and we had fantastic cold smoked fish and ribs all week.

The smoker is a backyard chef's straightest route to long-cooked barbecue—from smoked pork butt to simulate North Carolina barbecue to Texas-style beef brisket.

Fish is reason enough to invest in a special smoke oven. Smoke fish, cool it, and bring it forth for snacks or mini-meals. Sliver or flake it and put it on a cracker with fresh mayonnaise and a squeeze of lemon. Home-smoked fish heated in butter and piled on toast is a fine breakfast.

The fish is cured in brine for several hours or overnight. But smoking time for fillets is a mere 1 1/2 to 2 hours, in contrast to 4 to 12 hours for meat. After brining, the fish can be seasoned with coarse black pepper, multicolored peppers, herbs (tarragon, dill, sage, or rosemary), and/or garlic. Any fish, except delicate sole and flounder, benefits from smoking. The gentle moist heat firms up the texture of soft fish such as mullet.

Vegetables are a revelation—corn on the cob, whole roasted eggplant, peppers, tomatoes, and squashes, tasting of the food of ancient nomads. Smoke-baked sweet potatoes and russets gain new flavor. Dried beans cooked in an uncovered casserole will have a wonderful taste.

Smoke cooking has rich rewards, quite apart from the show quality of flipping food over a barbecue grill fire. The mysterious, rather primitive flavor is in fashion. Smoked food holds well in a refrigerator, so a summer weekend smoke-off provides first-class fare for a while.

HOW TO SMOKE MEATS AND MORE

Buy a smoker if you have space for it and want smoked foods often. The drum, firebox, water pan, and racks are in place for easy handling. In the fifties at the height of the do-it-yourself craze, hunters and fishermen made smokers of discarded oil drums, refrigerators, black iron stoves standing on three legs, or other salvage. These were ramshackle devices, blots on otherwise pretty gardens, but I still remember the fantastic smoked marlin and Florida boar that we sampled from time to time.

A hooded grill, charcoal-fueled or gas, can be converted to slow smoking. The cover must fit firmly, not airtight. Moisture in the smoke insures safety and keeps meat moist and tender. If you use a grill, push the coals aside and place a water pan in the firebox below the spot the meat will occupy on a rack.

Heat: Preheat an electric smoker or gas grill, setting heat at low to moderate on a gas grill. To use charcoal briquets, start the fire 30 to 45 minutes before cooking, to allow sooty smoke to burn away. When glowing coals are covered with gray ash, add briquets, a good handful for fish or chicken pieces, and enough to mound on the fire for a hunk of meat, turkey breast, whole bird, or roast. Keep the grill or smoker covered to heat it.

To start: The heat gauge on a smoker registers "ideal" or "medium" when the drum is hot enough to begin. Work quickly in placing foods on racks so that the cover is off as briefly as possible. Heat escapes rapidly when a smoker is opened. Spray the racks with nonstick vegetable spray or lay the food on lettuce leaves to prevent sticking. Arrange the food on racks, putting roasts on the lower rack, as they require longer smoking, whereas fish or chicken pieces are removed earlier. Space the pieces of food slightly apart to allow circulation of smoke.

Seasoning: Smoked foods are seasoned by marinades, but are drained before placing them on a rack. Seasonings also are introduced in the steam from the water pan. Add a cupful or two of the marinade to the pan and fill

SMOKING ALMOST ANYTHING

it with water. Or toss in appropriate herbs, fresh or dried: dill, oregano, tarragon (for chicken or fish), rosemary, mint (for lamb), or spices such as cinnamon or ginger, orange or lemon rinds, or garlic with pork or poultry. These aromatics will waft steamy smoke into the food.

To smoke: Cover the smoker. Smoke, moderate heat, and time do the work. Open the side door in the drum about once an hour, and add charcoal at the edges, if needed. If too much is added at once, black smoke will billow up and coat the food with soot. For long smokes, charcoal briquets can be started in another charcoal grill, then added at the edge of the smoker fire, using tongs and a poker to mix in coals. Check the pan occasionally and add fresh water if needed to keep it from cooking dry. The pan will sizzle when it boils dry.

To finish: Estimate your cooking time by the way a comparable piece of meat is timed in your smoker's manual or in a recipe here. About 45 minutes before the cooking time is up, sprinkle dampened chips or barbecue chunks onto fire, if wanted. Continue cooking until the total cooking time has elapsed. Test meat with a thermometer. It should register 160 degrees internal temperature for red meat or 180 degrees for poultry. Smoked meat can be cooked to the rare stage only if it is to be eaten immediately or if any leftovers will be finished the next day—the same as the rules for freshly roasted meat.

Alternate finish: Meat smoked two-thirds of the estimated smoking time can be finished in the oven, and it will retain much of its flavor and texture. Place the hot smoked meat on a rack in an open pan. Roast in a preheated 325-degree oven for an hour to an hour and a half, until a meat thermometer registers 160 for red meat or 180 for poultry.

To serve: Cool meat 30 minutes, slice thin, and serve warm or wrap in foil or plastic film and refrigerate overnight, then serve.

CHIPS, CHUNKS, OR PLUGS

Smoke aroma is provided by dampened chips, chunks, or plugs put on the fire 30 to 45 minutes before food will be removed from the smoker. Chips or chunks are cut from sweet woods such as hickory, red oak, mesquite, nutwoods, and fruitwoods. In wine country, plugs cut from discarded wine barrels are now packaged for smoke fires.

Chips, chunks, or plugs should be soaked for a half hour or so, until thoroughly moistened, before adding them to the fire. For a charcoal fire, place the moistened wood on top and it will steam and smoke fragrantly for about half an hour.

Soak a handful of chips in water in a bowl or bucket, ladle them out of the water with a small shovel or spatula, and scatter them over the fire so as not to smother it. For a fire 12 to 16 inches in diameter, soak two or three chunks or plugs and place them near the top of the fire.

To add fragrant wood chips or chunks to a gas grill with lava rocks, wrap moistened chips or chunks in a double thickness of aluminum foil, folded so an end of the packet is open. For steak, fish, chicken, or fast-cooking food, lay the packet on the rim of the fire with the open end turned toward the food before starting to cook. For long-cooked food, put the packet in place 20 to 30 minutes before cooking time is up.

WOODSY FRAGRANCE

Hickory and other nutwoods typically scent Dixie barbecue. Mesquite from the Southwest and California became the rage in the mid-eighties, and trendy chefs started smoking just about everything over mesquite. Home chefs followed suit, using logs where a few chips would do. Once a semipest in dry Western lands, mesquite became expensive and scarce. Grilled fish, fowl, and beast reeked of mesquite.

Now mesquite is reserved for beef, lamb, and, on occasion, pork or poultry. Alder was traditional for salmon in the Northwest for centuries and remains so. Fruitwoods, maple, hickory, and nutwoods are back for fish, chicken, and other birds. Grape vine trimmings cook fish and small steaks in France and vineyard regions everywhere. Barbecue chefs in Santa Maria, California, a farming community north of Santa Barbara, consider native red oak essential to seared juicy steaks. In South Florida, longtime barbecuers trim sprays from Australian pines (casuarina—a hardwood with leaves resembling pine) to throw on the fire to finish ribs, chicken, or beef.

In the North dogwoods and other ornamental hardwoods felled in winter storms are dried and salvaged by thrifty cooks for summer barbecues. Wineries and distilleries sell plugs cut from used barrels for barbecue smoking.

Any sweet hardwood is suitable, but never use resinous pine or evergreen. These woods imbue food with an acrid turpentine taste. Pine knots are called fat wood for their oily resin and make good fire starters, but be sure to let the resin burn away and the charcoal turn to glowing coals covered with gray ash, if you have used evergreen as kindling.

Avoid potentially poisonous woods such as oleander and native poisonwoods. The smoke causes rashes or other unpleasant reactions to sensitive persons hanging around the fire.

SMOKING ALMOST ANYTHING

SMOKED PORK BUTT WITH SMOKY APPLE CHUTNEY

Apple butter could be cooked in place of chutney, but the chutney is a stylish side dish with pork and leftovers—a great relish to keep in the refrigerator for another pork or poultry dinner later.

½ cup *each* cider vinegar, dry white wine, and water

½ medium-size onion, minced

2 cloves garlic, minced

2 tablespoons (½ ounce) yellow mustard seeds

2 (2-inch) cinnamon sticks, broken

1 pork butt, boned and rolled, about 5 pounds

½ teaspoon coarse black pepper

Smoky Apple Chutney (recipe follows)

Makes 8 servings, with leftovers.

Mix vinegar, wine, water, onion, garlic, mustard seeds, and cinnamon in ½-gallon plastic food storage bag. Place upright in bowl and lower pork butt into it. Seal and marinate 6 hours or overnight in refrigerator.

Fire: About 45 minutes before beginning to smoke meat, build fire in smoker pan, mounding charcoal briquets high after fire is started. Put water pan in place. Drain marinade from meat and pour into pan and fill with water.

Rub pork with pepper and place on lower rack of smoker. Cover smoker and begin smoking pork while mixing chutney.

Place chutney in large pan on upper rack and continue to smoke for a total of 5 hours. Stir chutney occasionally and, if needed, add more water to keep moist but not watery. Pork probably will not be completely done. Test with a meat thermometer. If pork has 160 degrees internal temperature and juices have no tinge of red, it is done and needs no further cooking.

To finish, place meat on rack in shallow pan. Brush with juices from chutney. Roast in oven heated to 325 degrees until internal temperature reaches 160 degrees. Cool slightly, slice thin, and serve with chutney.

SMOKY APPLE CHUTNEY

4 pounds Golden Delicious or other apples that
hold their shape, peeled and sliced thin

1 large red or green bell pepper, seeded and diced

2 large yellow onions, diced

1 large clove garlic, minced

1 2-inch piece fresh ginger, minced or thinly sliced

2 tablespoons (½ ounce) yellow mustard seeds

½ cup cider vinegar

¼ cup water

1 cup brown sugar, packed

¾ cup raisins (½ 9-ounce package) or currants

*Makes
2 quarts.*

Spray a stainless steel or enamelware Dutch oven with vegetable spray to make smoke easy to wash off after smoking. Combine all ingredients in pot. Stir to mix. Place on top rack of smoker. Cover smoker and smoke 4 to 5 hours, stirring chutney occasionally. Add more water if needed. Any leftovers can be stored in covered jars in refrigerator for several weeks.

SMOKED PORK CAROLINA STYLE

This resembles authentic Carolina barbecue pork more than the grilled pork on page 30, and we think the time spent smoking the meat is worth it once in a while.

Carolina Barbecue Sauce (page 190)

1 boned and tied pork shoulder, 3 to 4 pounds

Buns, split and buttered

Eastern Carolina Coleslaw (page 249)

Makes 12 to 15 barbecue sand-wiches.

Build fire in water smoker 30 to 45 minutes before starting pork to smoke. Pour 2 cups barbecue sauce in water pan, fill with water, and put in place. After smoker reaches cooking temperature, place pork on rack, brush liberally with sauce, put cover on smoker, and smoke 5 to 6 hours, basting with sauce and turning from side to side to color evenly every 20 to 30 minutes. Keep fire burning hot enough to hold smoker temperature at cooking level.

When thermometer inserted in center of pork butt registers 140 degrees, baste pork with sauce and place in shallow pan. Continue roasting in conventional oven heated to 325 degrees for 1½ hours, until internal temperature of meat is 165 degrees and meat almost falls apart. Cool meat slightly and shred it. Serve on buns with coleslaw.

COCHINITA PIBIL

"Little pig" marinated and roasted in a "pibil," a pit fired with wood coals, is typical of Yucatan. Tourists will find pibil-roasted pork in first-class restaurants in Merida, the capital city.

Traditionally the pork is wrapped in banana leaves, but corn husks, cabbage or other edible greens work as well. If your florist has banana leaves that have not been sprayed, use them. And foil works almost as well. The meat should be wrapped almost airtight to keep it moist and hold in the flavors of the marinade.

YUCATAN–STYLE PORK

1 tablespoon sliced garlic
2 teaspoons salt
½ cup orange juice
1 tablespoon white or cider vinegar
½ cup mild or medium salsa
1 boned and rolled pork butt, about 5 pounds
Green corn husks, banana leaves, or cabbage leaves
Peel of 1 orange, fresh or dried
4 or 5 cloves garlic
2 dozen corn tortillas

*Makes
10 to 12
servings.*

Several hours before cooking, work garlic with salt in bowl with spoon or mortar with pestle until pasty, then stir in orange juice, vinegar, and salsa. Place pork on leaves, laid overlapping to wrap meat well, and rub marinade over meat. Wrap and tie to hold in marinade. Place in plastic bag, close bag, and marinate in refrigerator 3 to 4 hours.

Build large fire in water smoker 30 to 45 minutes before cooking. Place orange peel and garlic cloves in water pan, fill with water, and put pan in place. Remove meat from bag and check leaf wrap as it protects meat while smoking. When smoker reaches cooking temperature, place pork in leaves on rack. Cover smoker, and smoke 5 to 6 hours. Feed fire as needed to hold smoker at cooking temperature.

When thermometer inserted in center of pork butt registers 140 degrees, transfer pork with leaf wrapping to rack in shallow pan. Continue roasting in conventional oven heated to 325 degrees for 1½ hours, until internal temperature of meat reaches 165 degrees and meat almost falls apart. Cool slightly, shred or chop meat, and use as filling for tortillas. Roll up and serve. Or serve meat on plates with cornbread and Frijoles Refritos (page 218) as accompaniments.

OWENSBORO, BAR–B–Q
CAPITAL OF THE WORLD

This small Kentucky city looks and talks Southern, but is worth a detour off the interstate mainly for barbecued mutton, not a Southern favorite and almost disappeared in this country. It went out of style with the Diamond Jim Brady era of sumptuous dining, except in this stronghold.

Barbecue men order mutton through a local purveyor who contracts with growers in the West to feed lambs past the young adulthood stage for use in Owensboro.

Old Hickory B–B–Q at Frederica and 25th Street is home folks' favorite. Harl Foreman carries on the business that his great-grandfather, a blacksmith, started in 1918. A son, John, attending the University of Kentucky, plans to come into the business full time when he graduates.

Harl sells eight times as much mutton as anything else, and the blackboard lists pork; next best-seller, beef; and chicken. The mutton is sliced or shredded and served on a bun with a slice of pickle and onion.

Each May a barbecue festival draws 40,000 people to the Ohio River bank in Owensboro. In 1988, they consumed 10 tons of mutton and 3,000 chickens. Other barbecue places in Owensboro are Shady Rest, operated by Dick and Louise Griffith, and Moonlite Bar-B–Q Inn, run by the family of its founder, Hugh Bosley, Sr.

SMOKE–BARBECUED LAMB SHOULDER

Lamb shoulder, bone-in or rolled and boned, is good this way. Since this makes only enough for six or eight servings, smoke two shoulders for a large group or freeze some for later use, though smoked meats may lose flavor if frozen longer than a couple of months.

1 lamb shoulder, rolled, boned and tied, 3 to 4 pounds

2 cups beef or chicken broth

2 tablespoons Worcestershire sauce

1 tablespoon dark molasses

¼ cup cider vinegar

¼ cup tomato juice

1 teaspoon salt

¼ teaspoon freshly ground pepper

6 to 8 buns, split, toasted and lightly buttered

2 large dill pickles, sliced

1 medium-size onion, sliced thin

Makes 6 to 8 servings.

Place lamb in plastic bag or deep bowl. Mix broth, Worcestershire, molasses, vinegar, tomato juice, salt, and pepper in bowl. Stir until salt is dissolved and sauce is blended. Pour marinade over lamb, close bag, or cover and marinate in refrigerator 6 to 8 hours or overnight.

Build large fire 30 minutes before cooking. Put water pan filled with water in place. Drain meat, reserving marinade. Place lamb on rack in smoker, cover smoker, and smoke 4 to 5 hours, until internal temperature reaches 120 degrees. Preheat oven to 325 degrees. Remove lamb to shallow baking dish and roast 1 to 1½ hours longer, until internal temperature reaches 160 degrees.

Serve while warm or chill and reheat to serve. Slice and serve on buns with pickle and onion in each sandwich.

CITRUS–PEEL TURKEY BREAST

Sliced smoked turkey breast goes fast at holiday parties, and is a treasure to have in the refrigerator in summer when it is too hot to cook.

TURKEY

1 6- to 7-pound turkey breast, thawed, if frozen

2 teaspoons salt

½ teaspoon coarse-ground black pepper

1½ teaspoons dried rosemary leaves

Corn, soy, or canola oil, for basting

Makes 12 to 14 servings.

FOR WATER PAN

2 ribs celery, cut in chunks

½ dried tangelo or Mandarin peel, broken in pieces

3 to 4 sprigs parsley

FOR CAVITY

2 green onions or scallions with tops, cut in
    2-inch pieces

1 rib celery, cut in 2-inch pieces

½ dried tangelo or Mandarin peel, cut in strips

3 sprigs parsley

Wipe turkey with paper towel. Rub with salt, pepper, and rosemary. Cover with plastic wrap and refrigerate while starting fire.

Start fire and add briquets until you have a mound of them. Burn until red-hot coals are covered with gray ash. Put water pan in place and fill with water, adding aromatic ingredients. Cover grill and preheat while preparing turkey.

Place turkey on square of doubled aluminum foil. Turn breastbone down and poke scallion, celery, citrus peel, and rosemary into cavity. Skewer skin flaps to breast to hold in filling, then carefully invert turkey with opening on foil square. Carefully transfer turkey to rack in smoker. Put turkey on bottom rack, shorter-cooking foods on upper rack.

Brush turkey skin lightly with oil. Cover smoker with lid—smoke will rise around the lid in about 10 minutes. As long as smoke is rising and thermometer on front registers medium heat to high heat, fire is hot enough. From time to time, add a few briquets at base of fire and poke them in. Do not allow fresh fuel to flame, as smoke deposits form soot on skin. Smoke 7 to 8 hours, until instant-reading thermometer registers 140 to 150 degrees.

Place hot turkey on rack in shallow roasting pan. Bake in 325-degree oven 30 to 45 minutes, until thermometer reads 155 degrees. Slice thin and serve warm or wrap in foil and refrigerate.

CITRUS PEEL

Dried citrus peel lends a touch of magic to the flavor of slow-cooked and smoked food. Dried peel goes in the cavity of a turkey or in a sauce for basting it and more peel goes in the water pan of the smoker.

In winter, dry the skin of slip-skin fruit such as tangelo or Mandarin orange. These so-called exotics are more pungent than ordinary oranges, though dried orange skins are good, too. Scoop the pulp from a half dozen pungent citrus shells. You need not scrape out the white pith, as its bitterness enhances the citrus flavor when the rind is cooked months later. Then put the rinds on waxed paper on a cool airy shelf and leave them to dry for about ten days in our North Carolina climate. In a cool, dry climate it will take less time; in a moist humid climate, more time. In a humid climate, if rinds show mold spots before they are dry, discard them and dry the next batch in a very low oven or one turned off after baking. Package each dried citrus shell in a tightly capped jar or plastic bag sealed well. Peel may turn dull brownish-orange, but brightens up when you cook it or soak it. If you don't have time to dry citrus rinds, shredded peel available in spice sections of markets is next best. Use 1/4 cup dry shredded peel for each citrus shell. Shredded Mandarin peel is available in many markets selling Oriental foods.

SMOKED CAPON

My friend Joe, butcher at Wellspring Grocery in Durham, North Carolina, talked me into smoking one of his fine capons. I didn't believe it could be so good. Yes, we fire up the smoker on snowy days when the results are so wonderful.

1 capon, 7 to 8 pounds

2 oranges, quartered

2 small onions, quartered

4 whole cloves

3 tablespoons butter

3 tablespoons Dijon-style mustard

1 tablespoon honey

2 tablespoons brandy or rum

Salt and freshly ground pepper to taste

Makes 8 to 10 servings, and left-overs are worth having around.

Rinse capon and pat dry. Squeeze juice of 1 orange over bird. Push shells of the juiced orange into cavity of bird along with 1 onion. Stud remaining onion with cloves and put in water pan with remaining orange. Fill water pan and put in place over hot fire in smoker.

Do not truss bird, as this deters cooking heavy joints at thighs. Place capon on rack in smoker and put on cover. Smoke 6 hours, adding charcoal as needed to keep smoker at cooking temperature. Meanwhile, beat together butter, mustard, honey, and brandy or rum with salt and pepper to taste (not too salty) until creamy. Transfer capon to small shallow pan or square of foil to catch drips of glaze and return to smoker. Spread with butter mixture and smoke 30 minutes longer. Transfer to 325-degree oven, baste with drippings from glaze, and roast to 180-degree internal temperature. Remove orange shells and onion from cavity and discard. Cool capon and serve warm, at room temperature, or refrigerate and serve cold. Slice thin and serve with baked sweet potatoes or wild and brown rice pilaf.

SMOKED PHEASANT LEGS

Smoked pheasant meat slivered off bones is stylish looking fanned out on a plate with a bowl of cranberry or apple sauce in the center. We serve it with thin toast as hors d'oeuvre or supper.

4 pheasant legs and 2 meaty back sections (see
    cutting instructions, page 135)

2 tablespoons red or white wine

2 tablespoons balsamic vinegar

1 clove garlic, minced

1 teaspoon *each* dried thyme and rosemary leaves

1 bay leaf, crumbled (rib removed)

1 tablespoon minced fresh or 1 teaspoon dried parsley

Olive oil

6 whole bay leaves

4 orange shells (left from fresh-squeezed juice)
    or 2 tablespoons slivered dried orange or tangerine
    peel

Makes 12 snack servings or 4 to 6 supper servings.

Place legs and backs in plastic bag. Mix wine, vinegar, garlic, thyme, rosemary, crumbled bay leaf, parsley, and olive oil in cup. Pour over pheasant. Seal bag, place in bowl, and refrigerate 3 to 4 hours.

Thirty minutes before smoking, build fire in water smoker. Fill water pan with water and add whole bay leaves and orange shells. Put in place in smoker.

Drain marinated legs and backs. Arrange on rack, with an inch or more of space between each. Cover and smoke 4 hours, until dry and brown. Test with instant-reading thermometer in thickest muscle of thigh. If not cooked to 180 degrees, place in baking dish, cover with foil, and roast at 325 degrees until 180 degrees internal temperature. Cool and refrigerate. Cut in slivers off bone to serve.

SMOKED LEMON ROSEMARY CHICKEN

Butterflied chicken lies flat on the grill to help it cook evenly and make carving simple: Remove wings and legs and carve across from neck end down. A two-rack smoker provides space for two chickens plus two or three fish fillets and a piece of cheese for guests to nosh on while they await the chicken. We have space for a vegetable, too—sweet potatoes when they are freshly dug in the early fall or corn in summer.

2 chickens, 2½ to 3 pounds each, butterflied
    (see below)
Salt and freshly ground pepper
3 lemons
2 tablespoons dried rosemary leaves or 4 tablespoons
    fresh
1 to 2 hickory chunks
Sweet Potatoes or Corn on the Cob (pages 243 and 184)

*Makes
8 to 10
servings.*

Have butcher butterfly chicken or do it this way: Pull away and discard visible fat from vent and neck openings. With sharp knife or sturdy scissors, cut close to one side of backbone from vent to neck opening. Cut along other side, keeping as close to bone as possible. Reserve backbone for making soup. Open the chicken out like a book. Snip membrane over breastbone. Place chicken bony side up on board. With heel of hand, whack breastbone smartly to loosen it. Pull out breast bone, cutting it from cartilage and flesh, if necessary. Discard it or use for soup.

Place chickens skin side up in large shallow dish. Season generously with salt and pepper. Cut the lemons and squeeze juice over chicken. Tuck lemon shells around chicken. Sprinkle with 1 tablespoon rosemary. Turn chickens in dish, cover with plastic film or foil, and refrigerate 2 to 6 hours.

Fire: About 45 minutes before beginning to smoke chicken, build fire in smoker pan, filling pan with charcoal. Put water pan in place. Place lemon shells from marinade and remaining 1 tablespoon rosemary in pan. Fill with water. Cover smoker and heat to smoking temperature.

Brush racks with oil and place a chicken skin side up on each rack, cover smoker, and smoke 4 hours, or until juices run clear when pierced with a fork. Do not lift cover except to add other foods to smoker.

Add charcoal at edge of fire or add hot coals from an auxiliary grill as needed to keep smoker hot. Add hickory chunks after 3½ hours.

Place chicken on platter. Cool 30 minutes before carving. Serve with Grill-Roasted Sweet Potatoes or Corn on the Cob.

SMOKED VENISON ROAST

*T*his works with farm-raised venison (see Shopping Sources, page 261) or
wild meat. Venison is lean, but water-smoking produces juicier meat than oven
roasting. This venison is best sliced paper-thin and served cold.

1 venison roast, tenderloin or sirloin preferred, or
      shoulder, 5 to 7 pounds
2 cloves garlic, cut in slivers
½ pound bacon, chopped fine
½ cup olive oil
Freshly ground pepper
1 cup dry red wine

*Makes
8 to 10
servings.*

Trim any skin or fat from meat. Cut slits at intervals in surface of
roast and fill with garlic and push in some of the chopped bacon. Brush
meat generously with oil and sprinkle heavily with pepper. Pour ½ cup
wine into water pan of smoker and fill with water. Put in place over hot
fire.

Place meat on rack in smoker. Cover with lid and smoke 5 hours,
feeding with a few charcoal briquets at a time to maintain cooking
temperature. Baste with remaining oil every hour, working quickly so as
not to disperse heat in smoker. Test internal temperature with thermometer.
It should be at 130 to 135 degrees. Place meat in large Dutch oven, add
remaining ½ cup wine, and simmer 45 minutes longer or until internal
temperature reaches 165 to 170 degrees. Serve hot with gravy (recipe
follows) or refrigerate and serve cold.

VENISON GRAVY

2 slices bacon
3 tablespoons flour
Pan juices from smoked venison
1 cup beef broth
Salt and pepper to taste

*Makes
1½ cups.*

Cut bacon in small pieces and sauté to render fat. Stir in flour. Add
pan juices and broth gradually, stirring until smooth and thickened. Taste
and add salt and pepper, if needed.

SMOKED SALMON WITH FENNEL

3 salmon fillets, 1 pound each

1 quart water

½ cup salt

1 large bulb fennel

Freshly ground pepper

Makes

12 to 15

appetizer

or snack

servings.

Place salmon in shallow dish or plastic bag. Combine water and salt in saucepan. Heat and stir until salt is dissolved. Cool and pour over salmon. If not sufficient to cover fish, prepare more brine. Cover and refrigerate overnight.

Remove salmon from brine and let dry on rack over waxed paper until glossy. This will take about 45 minutes, long enough to get the fire going.

Slice fennel from top to base thinly. Place fennel slices on rack of smoker. Place fish on fennel, put cover on smoker, and smoke 1½ to 2 hours, until salmon is no longer wet to the touch, just moist and slightly oily. Remove from smoker and cool or serve warm, sliced or flaked, on thin French bread or crackers. Wrap leftovers in plastic film and store up to 1 week.

PEPPERED CATFISH

Men, women, and children will all cluster around a tray of this smoked catfish with bread as they await the main event, which might be lemon chicken or pork butt with a vinegar and hot pepper sauce. Smoke the fish until it is firm if you are going to keep it for a week or so, or only until it barely becomes translucent at the thickest part, if you plan to serve it directly from the smoker to diners kibitzing about the smoke-chef's work.

2 catfish fillets, 8 ounces each

1 quart water

½ cup salt

2 lemons, cut in halves

1 tablespoon dried rosemary

2 lettuce or cabbage leaves

2 to 3 tablespoons coarsely ground black pepper

A few specks of crushed red pepper, optional

Lemon wedges, for garnish

Thin-sliced bread or whole-grain crackers

Makes 12 appetizer servings.

Place fish in a shallow baking dish or heavy plastic food bag. Stir together water and salt. Pour over fish, cover or seal bag, and soak several hours or overnight. Two hours before smoking, remove fish from brine, place on rack over waxed paper, and let dry until shiny.

Put lemon and dried rosemary (or 2 or 3 cupfuls Carolina Barbecue Sauce—page 190) in water pan and fill with water. Have heat at smoking temperature, with glowing coals covered with ash. Place a lettuce or cabbage leaf on grill at place where fish is to rest, place fish on leaves, rub with coarse black pepper and, if wanted, the red pepper flakes. Cover smoker, and let smoke 1½ hours for moist fish to serve within a day or two, about 2 hours for fish that is dryer and will keep refrigerated for a week or longer.

To serve, place fish on plate, garnish with greens if desired, and serve with lemon wedges and bread.

SMOKED SWEET POTATOES

Bake or microwave sweet potatoes in their skins until tender. Cut a cross in top of each, squeeze to push orange flesh up, and place potato on piece of foil on rack in smoker. Smoke 30 minutes.

Or, pierce skins of uncooked sweet potatoes and place each on a square of foil on rack about 1 hour before starting chicken. Smoke until soft, 4½ to 5 hours.

CORN ON THE COB

Buy corn with husks on it. Peel back husks carefully and remove silk. Brush kernals with melted butter or olive oil. Season lightly with a sprinkle of sugar and, if desired, dried herb such as thyme, marjoram, or dill. Pull husks up to cover corn and tie in place with twine. Smoke-cook 1½ hours. Serve hot with salt, any desired seasonings, and butter.

SMOKED GARLIC OR LEMON NUTS

Cocktail nut addicts think a smoker is worth its price for these nuts. Genuine smoked nuts are a considerable improvement over the chemically smoked nuts that come in jars and cans.

4 to 5 ounces cocktail almonds, walnuts, cashews,
    pecans, or peanuts for each 9-inch square pan
1 clove garlic, minced, or grated zest of 1 lemon

Spread nuts in pan wrapped in foil to protect it from smoke coating, or in disposable aluminum foil pan. Add seasoning and stir well. Spread nuts out and place on rack in smoker. (Nuts usually go in smoker with other foods, to occupy unused space.) Smoke 4 to 6 hours. Serve warm or cool and store in covered container.

SMOKED CHEESE

Cheeses smoked until oozy, and spread on thin-sliced French bread are grand wait food as meaty food is finishing. Mild-flavored cheeses—mozzarella, Edam, and Muenster—show smoky flavor dramatically, but Gruyère, Emmentaler, a good Cheddar, and exotic cheeses are good.

¼ pound cheese or ½ pound cut in 2 pieces
Heavy cream, olive oil, or Dijon-style mustard
Caraway seeds, rosemary, Italian seasoning, or
    other herbs

Place cheese in small ovenproof baking dish or on board that has been wrapped in aluminum foil to shield it from smoke. Or, after it is seasoned, cheese can be wrapped in foil pierced with holes to allow smoke to circulate.

Brush cheese with cream, oil, or mustard. Sprinkle with herbs. Leave cheese open or lightly wrap with foil pierced to allow smoke to circulate.

Place on top rack of water smoker to make checking cheese easy. Cover smoker and heat 45 minutes to 1 hour, until cheese is soft and seasoned with smoke. Remove foil from cheese and dish or board. Pass with cheese knives to spread cheese on bread. Allow ¼ pound for 3 people. Cheese loses its shape, but leftovers can be reheated to spread later and are good in salads.

SAUCES AND SEASONINGS

Three types of seasonings and sauces are used in barbecuing: dry seasonings that are rubbed on meat and poultry before grilling; marinades and basting sauces used before and during cooking; and table sauces brushed on just before food is taken from the grill, then passed at the table.

Brine or pepper water, hardly a sauce or marinade, is brushed on to moisten food while cooking. Fish and sometimes poultry are soaked in brine and dried before water smoking. Pepper water—just water and hot chiles—is brushed on pork or other meats at the start of cooking to keep them moist without introducing oily sauces at a stage when fats flare up and deposit sooty smoke on meats.

Granted, thousands of Americans barbecue

happily with commercial sauces and some are good. Upscale food magazines rated commercial sauces in boring repetition in the summer of '89. My quarrel with ratings is that many tasters had limited experience with barbecue and some tasted from a spoon. Barbecue sauce is only as good as the meat it flavors.

Choose a sauce to suit yourself, homemade or bottled. But don't be a one-sauce Joe. Barbecuing gets dull if it's all one taste.

DRY RUBS FOR BARBECUE

Basic dry rub can be kept in a jar to vary with additions from the spice shelf for barbecuing pork or poultry. The basic rub is used for beef.

BASIC DRY RUB

1/4 cup each salt, ground black pepper, and paprika

Put seasonings in a pint jar with tight-fitting lid, close jar, and shake vigorously to mix well. Store covered. This makes enough for 10 to 12 pounds chicken or pork ribs.

DRY RUB FOR RIBS

2 tablespoons Basic Dry Rub (above)

1 tablespoon sugar

1 teaspoon grated lemon peel

Makes 3 table- spoons.

Mix fresh just before using. Rub on ribs before barbecuing.

DRY RUB FOR POULTRY

2 tablespoons Basic Dry Rub (above)

1 teaspoon dry mustard

1 bay leaf, crumbled and rib removed, or 1 teaspoon
    leaf sage or rosemary leaves

1 clove garlic, minced

1 teaspoon grated lemon peel

Makes 3 table- spoons.

Mix fresh just before using. Rub on chicken or turkey before barbecuing. Makes enough for 6 to 8 pounds chicken or 2 large turkeys.

CAROLINA BARBECUE SAUCE

Carolinians are as chauvinistic about sauces as about basketball teams. Each region has its own.

EASTERN STYLE

1 pint cider vinegar

2 tablespoons salt

2 teaspoons ground red pepper

1 tablespoon red pepper flakes

2 tablespoons firmly packed brown sugar

Makes 1 pint.

Combine all ingredients, mix well, and let stand several hours before using.

PIEDMONT (LEXINGTON STYLE)

1½ cups cider vinegar

½ cup catsup

1 teaspoon salt

½ teaspoon ground red pepper

⅛ teaspoon red pepper flakes

1 tablespoon granulated sugar

½ cup water

Makes 1 pint.

Combine all ingredients in saucepan. Bring to a boil, then simmer and stir until sugar is dissolved. Cool and serve on meat.

WESTERN CAROLINA STYLE

1 cup catsup

1 cup firmly packed brown sugar

½ cup lemon juice

3 tablespoons butter or margarine

¼ cup minced onion

1 teaspoon hot pepper sauce

1 teaspoon Worcestershire sauce

Makes 1½ cups.

Place all ingredients in saucepan. Bring to a boil and simmer 30 minutes, or until slightly thickened.

SAUCE—EAST TO WEST

Regional preferences for sauces stir up virtual civil wars.
A map colored to reflect shades of regional barbecue sauce
would show Eastern North and South Carolina amber colored
for vinegar, butter, and hot peppers. Western North Carolina
favors a vinegary mix touched with catsup. Sauce on a pig
in Virginia might be either of these styles. Georgia is an
orange-red tint for catsup with mustard, onion, and vinegar.
Florida's catsup, butter, lime or lemon juice, and vinegar
sauce is ruddy-gold.

Sauces of Alabama, Mississippi, and Louisiana contain catsup or tomato-chili sauce, onion and garlic, vinegar,
sweetening, chiles or hot pepper, and Worcestershire sauces.
The basting and table sauce for mutton, pork, and beef in
Owensboro, Kentucky, is dark brown with Worcestershire,
tangy with vinegar, and lightly sweet. Color in Texas goes
dark red with chili sauce and occasionally coffee. Kansas City
sauce is dark brownish red, from spices and tomato.

Californians borrow and adapt from everywhere. Cal-
Mex sauce is zesty and tomatoey or a mild salsa. Hawaiian
influence dominates sweet-sour sauces with fruit juice, remi-
niscent of luaus of the fifties. Winemaker barbecuers put wine
in the sauce, which may be more herby than zesty.

FLORIDA BARBECUE SAUCE

One barbecue regular says this sauce originated in Jacksonville. I've had it in Miami, Georgia, and Alabama on ribs, chicken, beef, fish, and lobster. To me it is too pungent for fish, but great on pork, beef, or chicken. This makes enough for three to four quartered chickens or ten pounds of ribs.

1 stick (½ cup) butter or margarine

1 cup cider vinegar

1 cup catsup

1 (5- to 6-ounce) jar prepared horseradish

Juice of 6 lemons or limes

1 teaspoon salt

1 tablespoon Worcestershire sauce

1 teaspoon hot pepper sauce

Makes
3½ cups.

In a medium-size stainless steel or enamelware saucepan, melt butter. Add remaining ingredients. Bring to a boil and simmer uncovered 20 to 25 minutes. Use as basting sauce on pork, chicken, or other meats, and serve as a table sauce. Leftover sauce can be refrigerated and kept up to 2 or 3 weeks.

Note: If using this sauce on chicken, lemons are better than limes; limes give a sharp tang that suits pork or beef to a T.

GEORGIA BARBECUE SAUCE

Whole hogs or pork butts are basted lightly with this or a similar sauce in Georgia. Its sweet-spicy flavor perks up kitchen-grilled hamburgers or sausages, too. It makes enough for three to four chickens or four to five pounds pork.

1½ cups catsup
1 cup cider vinegar
⅓ cup vegetable oil
⅓ cup Worcestershire sauce
½ cup firmly packed brown sugar
3 tablespoons prepared yellow mustard
2 to 3 cloves garlic, minced
1 lemon, cut in halves

Makes about 3 cups.

In a saucepan, combine catsup, vinegar, oil, Worcestershire sauce, brown sugar, mustard, and garlic. Squeeze lemon juice into sauce and add 1 lemon half shell. Heat slowly about 10 minutes. Sauce does not have to reach the boil, but heating blends flavor. Use sparingly as basting sauce for fresh pork, ham, ribs, or chicken. Heat additional sauce and serve as a table sauce.

WESTERN BARBECUE SAUCE

Soy sauce provides flavor-mellowing smoothness to many barbecue sauces of the West. This recipe makes enough for three to four pounds meat.

¼ cup soy sauce
¼ cup catsup
½ cup dry red wine
2 tablespoons olive oil
1 small onion, chopped fine
1 teaspoon chili powder
1 teaspoon freshly ground pepper
1 clove garlic, minced

Makes 1¼ cups.

In a stainless steel or enamelware saucepan, combine all ingredients. Mix well and bring to a boil. Keep warm and brush lightly on lamb or beef while grilling. Leftover sauce can be boiled and served as table sauce.

TEXAS BARBECUE SAUCE

This sauce is served at table, spooned over meat or to the side for dipping each bite in. It also can be mixed with shredded pork or beef to make sandwiches. Do not cook with it.

½ stick (¼ cup) butter

1 small onion, chopped

1 clove garlic, minced

3 ribs celery, finely chopped

1 cup catsup

½ cup cider vinegar

1½ cups water

¼ cup Worcestershire sauce

3 bay leaves

1 teaspoon freshly ground pepper

1 tablespoon chili powder, or to taste

Makes 2 cups.

In a large stainless-steel or enamelware saucepan melt the butter. Add onion, garlic, and celery. Cook and stir until onion is tender. Stir in catsup, vinegar, water, and Worcestershire sauce. Add bay leaves and pepper. Simmer uncovered 15 to 20 minutes, stirring now and then to prevent sticking. Stir a small amount of sauce into chili powder and blend well. Stir chili mixture into sauce. Remove bay leaves. Let stand at room temperature 1 hour or longer before serving. Leftover sauce can be refrigerated for several days.

A WORD ABOUT SAUCES
IF OLD RECIPES DON'T WORK

Sauces used on gas grills and some covered grills should be lean. Grills of the fifties could be adjusted high to allow fat to drizzle on the coals to enhance flavor, not cause a conflagration. Recent model gas grills and covered grills with limited flexibility are too close to accept grease without flaring back.

BONE–BROTH BASTING SAUCE

*O*ld-time chefs call beef broth bone-broth—too often overlooked as a meaty-flavored ingredient in a basting sauce—as for them it started with a good soup bone. This sauce can be used on beef or ribs. For lamb, make lamb broth of lamb stew meat and bones.

1 teaspoon salt

1 teaspoon dry mustard

1 bay leaf, finely crumbled

1 teaspoon chili powder, or to taste

1/2 teaspoon paprika

1 teaspoon hot pepper sauce

1/2 cup Worcestershire sauce

1/2 cup cider vinegar

3 cups beef broth, canned or homemade

1/3 cup oil

1 tablespoon soy sauce

1 clove garlic, crushed

Makes 4 1/2 cups, enough to baste about 5 pounds meat.

In a stainless-steel or enamelware saucepan blend salt, mustard, bay leaf, chili powder, and paprika. Slowly stir in pepper and Worcestershire sauces to dissolve mustard, then stir in vinegar, beef broth, soy sauce, and garlic. Bring to a boil. Let cool, pour into a jar, cover, and refrigerate overnight before using. Brush on beef, pork, or lamb for barbecuing. Leftover sauce takes on the smoky flavor of the meat, so some chefs think it even better the next time around. Refrigerate any leftover sauce and use within a few days or freeze.

LOUISIANA BARBECUE SAUCE

Brush this sauce on just during the last 10 minutes of grilling ribs, chicken, or beef, as it burns easily. The sauce then goes to the table to be spooned over the meat.

1 cup each olive and vegetable oils

4 large onions, finely chopped

1 large green pepper, seeded and diced

1 rib celery, finely chopped

1 (8-ounce can) tomato sauce

¾ cup catsup

1 teaspoon prepared mustard, preferably Creole-style

1 tablespoon vinegar

3 to 4 drops liquid smoke (optional)

Makes 4½ cups, enough for 10 to 12 pounds meat.

In a large stainless-steel or enamelware saucepan heat the oils. Add onions, green pepper, and celery and cook until onions are lightly browned. Stir in tomato sauce, catsup, mustard, vinegar, and liquid smoke, if using. Simmer 10 to 15 minutes.

ORANGE PEEL BARBECUE SAUCE

Citrus grove workers often keep a couple of orange peels drying on a high shelf in the pantry. You can do this, too, if you save a peel cleaned of its pith and juice; when it becomes leathery it is ready to use. You can buy dried orange peel in Oriental food markets, too.

1 tablespoon slivered or grated dried orange peel

¼ cup each catsup, soy sauce, and orange juice

1 tablespoon honey

2 tablespoons oil

1 teaspoon freshly ground pepper

Makes ⅓ cup.

Combine all ingredients. Use as a marinade and basting sauce for pork, chicken, or beef.

CHICKEN–COUNTRY BARBECUE SAUCE

Versions of this sauce are used in mass chicken barbecues put on by poultrymen in the East and some other parts of the country. Pure grilled chicken flavor predominates with seasonings applied discreetly, as here.

1 egg
1 cup vegetable oil
2 cups cider vinegar
1 teaspoon salt
1½ teaspoons poultry seasoning, dried marjoram,
    or minced parsley
½ teaspoon freshly ground pepper

Makes enough sauce for 2 to 3 chickens.

Beat egg in medium-size bowl, then beat in oil until well blended. Stir in vinegar, salt, herb, and pepper. Place chicken halves or quarters on grill and sear on both sides. Brush lightly with sauce and grill 45 minutes to 1 hour, turning and brushing lightly with sauce every 10 to 15 minutes. Leftover sauce should be refrigerated and used within 2 or 3 days.

ROADSIDE BARBECUE

The Delmarva Peninsula, which protects the Chesapeake Bay from the Atlantic on the East, is chicken country and summer beach land. Roadside barbecues along beach roads feed tourists and homefolk happily with a distinctive sort of chicken barbecue.

Shacks are erected each season by roadside barbecuers and are taken down before wintry weather comes. The barbecue "pits" are masonry structures with heavy metal mesh grids or kettle-type cookers made of oil drums cut in halves with metal grills to support the chicken.

The fire burns slowly to cook chicken golden and tender. The sauce is simply oil and vinegar with seasonings, and often an egg to give chicken a shiny golden glaze.

Summer people keep eyes cocked for signs that announce roadside barbecues a few hundred yards before the highway turnoff. Families pile out of cars to order lunch or dinner, to take along as a beach picnic, to eat at home, or at a vacation cottage for lunch or dinner. A typical barbecue plate contains a half chicken, French fries, and coleslaw.

ALL-PURPOSE WINE SAUCE

This sauce complements meat, poultry, or fish if you match the wine to the food—white for fish or light poultry, red for meat. It contains no sweetening or tomato, so is less likely to burn than most sauces

¾ cup red, white, or rosé wine

½ cup red or white wine vinegar

¼ cup olive oil

1 cup minced chives or scallion tops

1 cup minced parsley

2 cloves garlic, minced

1 teaspoon salt

1 teaspoon freshly ground pepper

1 tablespoon soy sauce

Makes

about

2 cups.

This sauce is best prepared the day before barbecuing. In a large glass bowl or jar mix all ingredients, cover tightly, and let stand overnight at room temperature to blend flavors. Use as basting sauce for beef, pork, lamb, poultry, fish, or game or as marinade. Leftover sauce should be refrigerated, as meat drippings will have been mixed into it with the basting brush.

PICO DE GALLO

This sauce is traditional as a spread for warm tortillas. An experienced Texan or other fire-eater will fill and roll up a warm tortilla this way so it doesn't drip: Lay the tortilla flat on the hand, spread a bit (or more) of sauce on it, then fold up the right side of it, and roll toward you to encase the sauce.

1 whole jalapeño, or more to taste

½ cup minced cilantro leaves

1 large clove garlic, minced

1 bunch green onions or scallions, sliced thin

1½ cups chopped, peeled, and seeded tomatoes or
    drained canned tomatoes

2 avocados, peeled and diced

½ teaspoon salt, or to taste

⅛ teaspoon black pepper

Makes 2½ cups.

Seed and mince jalapeños. Combine with cilantro, garlic, green onions, and tomatoes in small bowl. Mix well. Add avocados and mix lightly. Stir in salt and pepper. Chill for 2 or 3 hours before serving.

CILANTRO—YES OR NO?

There's no middle road about cilantro. You either love it or detest it. The sharp weedy taste cuts the fire and spice of guacamole and countless other U.S.-Mex foods perfectly to some of us. Others get the taste of something bad permeating the familiar Tex-Mex food. Cilantro is foliage of the coriander plant, but coriander seeds taste only faintly of the fresh gray-green leaves.

Another name for cilantro is Chinese parsley. It is used in Southeast Asian, East Indian, and Central and South American cookery. You find it fresh year round from greenhouses or hydroponic farms, but in-season field-grown cilantro has better flavor and color. It wilts and dies in humid weather, so in summer locally grown cilantro is scarce. It grows in pots with well-drained soil, but seeds are slow to germinate.

And try it in a Tex-Mex restaurant before devoting a lot of time and money to cultivating it or going on a shopping trek for it. But some of us think it worth the effort to have it as a garnish, its main function.

CLASSIC SOY MARINADE

This sauce perks up pork, beef, lamb, or poultry and can be used for conventional broiling and roasting. I put a flank steak in this sauce to marinate before I go to the office, and grill it when I get home. You'll have enough sauce for three to four pounds chicken or two to three pounds fish.

1/2 cup soy sauce

1/4 cup dry white wine

2 tablespoons brown sugar

3 or 4 thin slices fresh ginger root, or 1/2 teaspoon
    ground ginger

2 cloves garlic, minced

Makes

3/4 cup.

Combine all ingredients and mix well. Pour over meat and marinate at room temperature 30 minutes or in refrigerator overnight.

DILL–LEMON BASTING SAUCE

This is obviously for fish, but try it on chicken and lamb, too.

1/2 cup lemon juice

2 tablespoons butter

1 tablespoon chopped fresh dill, or 1 teaspoon dill weed

1/2 teaspoon salt

1/4 teaspoon freshly ground pepper

Makes

enough

sauce for

2 to 3

pounds fish.

In a small saucepan combine lemon juice, butter, dill, salt, and pepper. Heat until bubbling. Cool to lukewarm before using. (Another way to make this is to soften the butter, then beat all the ingredients together to form a smooth cream flecked with dill.) Sprinkle on more fresh dill after cooking to emphasize the flavor, if you like.

FAST LITTLE SAUCE

We needed a sauce for a couple of pork chops when the cupboard was next to bare. We built this sauce from this and that. It perked up the pork chops, and worked out as a table sauce for chicken and beef, as well as pork.

2 tablespoons vegetable oil

2 tablespoon each diced onion and green bell pepper

2 cloves garlic, minced

1/2 cup each cider vinegar and catsup

1/4 cup Worcestershire sauce

1 tablespoon sugar

Makes about 3/4 cup.

Heat oil in skillet. Add onion and bell pepper. Cook and stir until onion is tender but not browned. Add garlic, stir well, then add vinegar, catsup, Worcestershire, and sugar. Simmer uncovered 15 minutes, until thickened, stirring now and then. Salt is not needed, since reducing the sauce concentrates the salt in the catsup and Worcestershire. Serve warm or cooled on pork, chicken, or beef. Can be used as basting sauce toward the end of cooking.

RAISINBERRY SAUCE

This sweet, holidayish sauce tends to burn, so keep it as a table condiment or precooking marinade for poultry or pork.

12 ounces (2¼ cups) golden raisins

2 cups orange juice

1 cup water

¼ cup lemon juice

1 cup sugar

12 ounces (3 cups) fresh or frozen cranberries

1 tablespoon grated orange peel

Makes

4½ cups.

In a large saucepan, combine raisins, orange juice, water, lemon juice, and sugar. Bring to a boil, stirring until sugar is dissolved, and simmer 10 minutes. Add cranberries and boil 5 minutes, or until berries start to pop. Add orange peel and simmer 5 minutes, or until sauce is reduced to a syrupy consistency. Cool. Pour into a large jar, cover, and refrigerate up to 1 month. Serve as a table sauce or use as a marinade for pork or poultry.

TOMATO BARBECUE SAUCE

1 medium onion, chopped

1 clove garlic, minced

2 tablespoons oil

2 (14½-ounce) cans tomatoes

2 ribs celery, finely chopped

1 bay leaf

3 tablespoons brown sugar

1 tablespoon prepared mustard

1 teaspoon hot pepper sauce

1 teaspoon salt

½ cup cider vinegar

1 teaspoon allspice

½ teaspoon ground cloves

Makes 3 cups, enough for 3 to 4 quartered broiler-fryers or 5 to 6 pounds pork.

In a stainless-steel or enamelware saucepan cook onion and garlic in oil until tender but not browned. Stir in tomatoes, celery, bay leaf, brown sugar, mustard, pepper sauce, salt, vinegar, allspice, and cloves. Cut up tomatoes, snipping through sauce with scissors. Bring to a boil, mashing tomatoes against sides of pan to chop more. Simmer uncovered 30 minutes. Remove from heat and discard bay leaf. If smoother sauce is preferred, puree in blender or food processor, making sure top of container is tightly closed so no hot sauce can spatter out. Use to baste chicken or pork and as a table sauce.

LEMON BUTTER

Butter sauces lift good grilled steak, fish, or chicken to gastronomic heights. These compounds are essentially table sauces, but are used sparingly to moisten simple foods while grilling.

1 stick (½ cup) butter, softened
1 teaspoon grated lemon peel
Juice of ½ lemon

Makes
4 to 6
servings.

Beat butter until fluffy. Gradually beat in lemon peel and juice until throughly incorporated. Drop a spoonful of sauce on each serving.

ANCHOVY BUTTER

1 stick (½ cup) butter, softened
3 to 4 flat anchovy fillets, mashed
½ teaspoon lemon juice
Freshly ground pepper

Makes
4 to 6
servings.

Beat butter until fluffy. Beat anchovies, lemon juice, and pepper into butter. Serve at room temperature as sauce for grilled fish or lamb.

CAPER BUTTER

1 stick (½ cup) butter, softened
2 tablespoons capers, chopped fine if large
½ teaspoon caper juice
½ teaspoon lemon juice
Freshly ground pepper

Makes 8
servings.

Beat butter until fluffy. Beat in capers and juice, lemon juice, and pepper to taste. Serve chilled or at room temperature as dressing for fish, pork, or lamb.

SAGE BUTTER

1 stick (½ cup) butter, softened
2 tablespoons minced fresh or 1 teaspoon dried
    sage leaves
1 tablespoon minced fresh parsley
Juice of ½ lemon
Salt and freshly ground pepper

Makes 4 to 6 servings.

Beat together butter, sage, and parsley until fluffy and well blended. Beat in lemon juice, salt, and pepper. Cover and chill 30 minutes. Drop spoonfuls onto grilled pork, chicken, or turkey.

SHALLOT–PARSLEY BUTTER

2 tablespoons minced shallots
1 tablespoon minced fresh parsley, preferably flat-leaf
¼ cup dry white wine
1 stick (½ cup) butter, softened
Salt and freshly ground pepper

Makes 4 to 6 servings.

In a small skillet combine shallots, parsley, and wine. Bring to a boil and boil briskly until wine has almost evaporated. Watch carefully to prevent burning. Cool thoroughly. In a small bowl, beat butter until fluffy. Beat in the shallot-parsley mixture, salt, and pepper until well blended. Serve spoonfuls on grilled steaks, pork, or poultry.

GREEN BUTTER

1 stick (½ cup) butter, softened
¼ cup minced watercress
1 tablespoon minced fresh parsley
1 tablespoon minced scallion tops
Juice of ½ lemon
Salt and freshly ground pepper

Makes
4 to 6
servings.

In a small bowl combine butter, watercress, parsley, and scallion tops. Beat until fluffy and well blended. Beat in lemon juice, salt, and pepper. Cover and chill 30 minutes. Drop by spoonfuls onto grilled fish, poultry, or other meats.

JANE TRUMBULL'S TARTAR SAUCE

Jane Trumbull whipped up this unusually delicate sauce for fish when her husband, Steve, grilled Spanish mackerel.

1 stick (½ cup) butter
Juice of 2 large limes
About ⅓ cup mayonnaise
6 scallions with tops, minced

Makes
about
1 cup.

In a small saucepan melt butter. Stir in lime juice and beat in mayonnaise to make a smooth sauce that just barely holds a mound when dropped from a spoon. Stir in scallions. Serve at room temperature with grilled or fried fish.

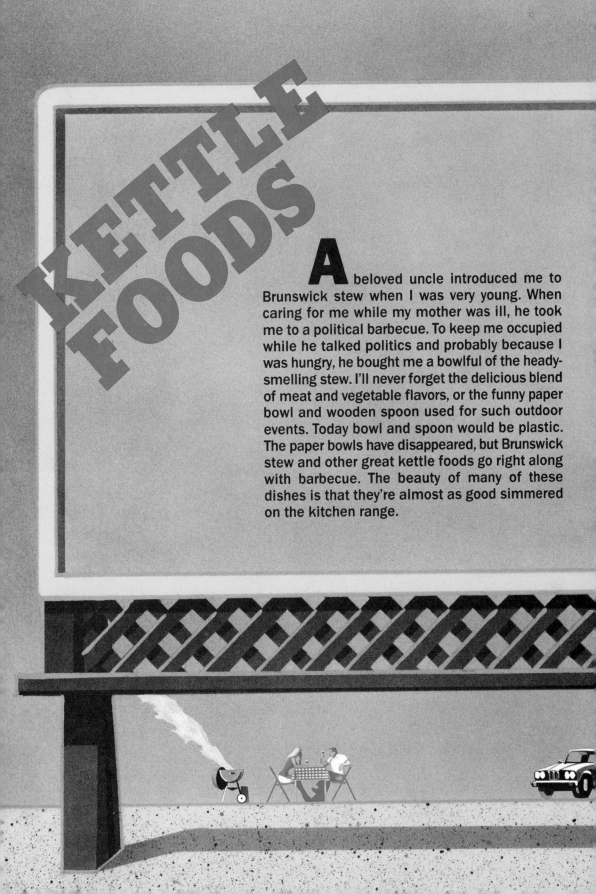

KETTLE FOODS

A beloved uncle introduced me to Brunswick stew when I was very young. When caring for me while my mother was ill, he took me to a political barbecue. To keep me occupied while he talked politics and probably because I was hungry, he bought me a bowlful of the heady-smelling stew. I'll never forget the delicious blend of meat and vegetable flavors, or the funny paper bowl and wooden spoon used for such outdoor events. Today bowl and spoon would be plastic. The paper bowls have disappeared, but Brunswick stew and other great kettle foods go right along with barbecue. The beauty of many of these dishes is that they're almost as good simmered on the kitchen range.

BRUNSWICK STEW

There are as many versions of Brunswick stew as there are barbecue chefs or their wives. This recipe is adapted from a famous woman cook in my small hometown, Montevallo, Alabama. The lemon gives a snap of flavor, and I have cut sugar, catsup, and other old-fashioned flavors from the formula.

3 pounds broiler-fryer legs or 1 stewing chicken, 3½ pounds

1 pound boneless lean pork, rib end or shoulder

6 cups water, or as needed

2 large onions, coarsely chopped

1 cup sliced celery

3 medium potatoes, peeled and diced

1 lemon, sliced and seeded

¼ cup Worcestershire sauce

1 tablespoon prepared yellow or brown mustard

2 teaspoons salt, or to taste

1 (14½-ounce) can tomatoes, or 2 cups peeled and chopped fresh tomatoes

1½ pounds green baby lima beans, shelled, or 1 (10-ounce) package frozen

2 cups corn cut off cobs, or 1 (10-ounce) package frozen whole-kernel corn

Makes 10 to 12 side-dish servings or 6 to 8 main-dish servings.

In a large kettle, combine chicken and pork with water to barely cover. Cover kettle and simmer until chicken and pork are very tender, 1 hour for broiler-fryer legs, 1½ to 2 hours for stewing chicken. Remove chicken from broth, discard skin and bones, and return meat to broth. Remove pork and cut in chunks, discarding fat and cartilage. Return meat to broth. I like chicken and pork in recognizable pieces, but meat is sometimes shredded.

Add onions, celery, potatoes, lemon, Worcestershire sauce, mustard, and salt. Cover and simmer 15 minutes, until potatoes are almost tender. Add tomatoes, limas, and corn. Cover and simmer 15 minutes, or until limas are tender. Remove lemon. Serve hot in large soup bowls. Brunswick stew may be served over rice, though it is served simply with saltines when it accompanies barbecue.

KENTUCKY BURGOO

Kentuckians tell you that burgoo goes with barbecue, but in Louisville I've also had it for a Derby breakfast—along with country-smoked ham, grits soufflé, and hot biscuits.

1 stewing chicken, 3 to 3½ pounds

2 pounds beef shank

1 pound lamb or veal stew meat

4 quarts water

1 tablespoon salt, or to taste

1 teaspoon freshly ground black pepper

½ teaspoon cayenne pepper, or to taste

4 medium potatoes, peeled and cubed

1 large onion, diced

1 cup peeled and chopped carrots

½ cup minced fresh parsley

2 (14½-ounce) cans tomatoes, chopped

2 cups shelled baby lima beans, or 1 (10-ounce)
    package frozen

2 medium green peppers, seeded and chopped

3 cloves garlic, minced

1 pound okra, sliced

4 cups corn cut off cobs, or 2 (17-ounce) cans
    whole-kernel

Makes about 30 side-dish servings, 20 main-dish servings.

In a 9-quart or larger kettle combine chicken, beef, lamb or veal, water, 2 teaspoons salt, black and cayenne peppers. Cover and simmer 2 hours or until chicken and meat are very tender. Remove meats from broth. Remove and discard skin and bones from chicken and bone from beef and shred the meats. Return to broth. Add potatoes, onion, carrots, parsley, tomatoes, limas, green peppers, and garlic. Mix and bring to a boil, turn heat low, and simmer 1½ hours, stirring often to prevent sticking. Add okra and corn and simmer 20 to 30 minutes longer. Taste and add more salt and pepper, if needed. Add more cayenne, too, if not spicy enough; burgoo should be tangy, but not really hot. Serve in soup cups as a side dish to barbecued pork, mutton, lamb, chicken, or beef, or in soup plates as a supper main dish.

KETTLE BARBECUE PORK

North Carolinians barbecue pork in the air-conditioned comfort of their kitchens occasionally with pork butt cooked this way.

Hickory chips, soaked
1 pork butt, preferably boned and tied, 5 to 6 pounds
Carolina Barbecue Sauce, Eastern or Western Style
    (page 190)
Sandwich buns, split, toasted and buttered

Makes 10 to 12 sand- wiches.

Push coals to back of grill and put drip pan in place. Spread chips over fire and place pork butt over drip pan. Grill and smoke 1 to 1½ hours. Place hot pork in slow cooker or large kettle. Add 1 cup sauce. Cover and simmer 4 to 5 hours, until meat falls off bone. Shred meat, using fingers, fork, and small knife. Discard skin and excess fat. Place meat in large bowl and mix in 1 cup more sauce. Pile on buns and serve more sauce on the side.

KETTLE BARBECUED BEEF

This classic Texas barbecue was served in priceless china soup plates at a dinner party the first time I had it. It is traditional everywhere—high school football banquets, teen-agers' gatherings, and ranch picnics. Liquid smoke is essential. I like a modest amount, but Texans use much more—up to a half bottle for this pot of beef.

1 point-cut brisket, 2½ to 3 pounds
¾ cup bottled chili sauce
¼ cup brown sugar, packed
2 tablespoons Worcestershire sauce
1 teaspoon hot pepper sauce, or to taste
1 (12-ounce) can beer
1 tablespoon liquid smoke, or to taste

Makes 5 to 6 large servings.

Place meat in a plastic bag. Combine chili sauce with brown sugar, Worcestershire and pepper sauces, beer, and liquid smoke. Stir until sugar is dissolved. Pour over meat. Close bag; turn to coat meat well and marinate at room temperature 1 hour or in refrigerator overnight.

Place meat and marinade in a Dutch oven or large deep skillet with cover. Cover tightly and bake at 300 degrees 3 to 4 hours, or simmer over very low heat until meat comes apart in shreds. Place on large warm platter with sauce, pull apart meat in shreds with fork, and serve on rice or split and toasted buns. Pinto beans are the customary accompaniment.

KETTLE BEEF BARBECUE ON BUNS

Kettle barbecue is made in enormous quantities for block parties, church suppers, and other large groups. The recipe is easily multiplied if you have a huge kettle and a hefty person to lift it.

1 pound ground lean beef

1 large onion, chopped

2 cloves garlic, minced

1 (6-ounce) can tomato paste

3 cups tomato juice

2 teaspoons to 2 tablespoons chili powder (some like it hot)

Salt to taste

2 teaspoons celery seed

1 tablespoon sugar

1 tablespoon Worcestershire sauce

1 tablespoon vinegar

Hot water as needed

1 (12-ounce) can corned beef, or 1½ cups shredded
    freshly cooked corned beef

6 to 8 sandwich buns, split and toasted

Makes

6 to 8

servings.

In a large heavy kettle, sauté beef, onion, and garlic until meat loses its red color, breaking up with a fork to keep crumbly. Pour off fat that collects, or siphon it off with a bulb baster and discard. Add tomato paste and juice, chili powder, ½ teaspoon salt, celery seed, sugar, Worcestershire sauce, and vinegar to meat mixture. Cover and simmer 1 hour, stirring from bottom now and then to prevent scorching. After 30 minutes, stir in 1 cup hot water or more if needed; sauce should have a stewlike but not watery consistency. Shred corned beef with fork and stir into sauce. Taste and add more salt, if needed. Serve on buns. This is eaten with fork and knife.

CHICKEN PILAU

*In north Florida and south Georgia, pilau is traditional with barbecue, picnic, and family reunion food. Pilau is one of the many food contributions of the Minorcans, the earliest remaining settlers of St. Augustine, but the English settlers from Georgia and other latecomers have changed the pronunciation of pilau to **per-loo**. Most pilaus are made fiercely hot with the tiny local chile, the datil pepper.*

1 tablespoon oil or chicken fat

2 medium onions, finely chopped

2 medium green peppers, seeded and finely chopped

3 ribs celery, finely chopped

2 pounds chicken thighs, or 1 broiler-fryer, cut up

5 cups chicken broth

1½ teaspoons salt, or to taste

½ teaspoon white pepper

1 jalapeño, datil (bird), or other hot pepper,
　　seeded and minced

1½ cups long grain rice

Makes 10 to 12 side-dish servings, 6 to 8 main-dish servings.

If you have homemade chicken broth in the freezer, fat from the broth can be skimmed for use in cooking the vegetables for pilau. Heat oil or fat in a large kettle, add onions, green peppers, and celery. Cook, stirring now and then, until onions are tender and translucent. Add chicken, broth, salt, and white pepper. Cover and simmer until chicken is very tender, 35 to 40 minutes.

Remove chicken from broth, remove skin and bones, and return chicken to broth. Add hot pepper and rice. Stir once, cover, bring to a boil, turn heat very low, and cook until most of liquid is absorbed and rice is tender, about 20 minutes. If rice cooks dry before it is tender, add ¼ cup hot water. If rice is too wet when done, uncover and cook over high heat to evaporate some of the liquid. Stir rice with a fork. Serve hot.

FRIED FISH AND HUSHPUPPIES

Frying fish in the back yard takes the onus off this sort of cooking. Any smell dissipates quickly outdoors and any grease spatters are washed away by rain, if they are even noticeable. In hot weather, this is the only sensible way to fry fish.

3 panfish or small fish fillets per person
Salt and freshly ground pepper
White corn meal, preferably water-ground
Oil, at least a 24-ounce bottle for fish for 6
Tallahassee Hushpuppies (page 239)
Lime or lemon wedges

Spread fish on an enamelware or plastic tray and sprinkle lightly with salt and heavily with pepper. Scatter corn meal over fish to coat well, turn fish, and repeat seasoning and coating. Have fire burned down to hot coals at one side of grill, with more coals at edge to poke into fire if needed for more heat.

Place skillet over hottest part of fire and pour in 1/2 inch oil. Heat until almost sizzling. Add fish in a single layer, being careful not to crowd it. Cook over medium-to-hot heat until lightly browned; turn and brown other side. Fish will not turn golden brown, only a pale tan-gold color. If browned, it probably is overcooked. As fish is cooked, remove to a tray lined with paper towels. Let drain while cooking remaining fish and hushpuppies. Add more oil as needed.

As the last batch of fish is fried, drop hushpuppies in. Poke fire to spread coals as you need a moderate heat for the little fried breads. Fry hushpuppies and drain on paper towels. Arrange fish and hushpuppies on plates and garnish with lime or lemon.

BLACK BEAN CHILI WITH TURKEY

Use pinto, red, or pink beans if you prefer, but black-bean chili is special. Broth from cooking the turkey legs makes a rich base for this all-American fare, fun to ladle from a kettle on a barbecue grill.

2 pounds turkey drumsticks or leg quarters

Water

1 carrot, peeled and cut in chunks

1 rib celery, cut in chunks

1 onion, peeled and studded with 2 whole cloves

1 bay leaf

3 teaspoons salt

1 teaspoon freshly ground pepper

1 pound black beans

1 green bell pepper, chopped

3 medium onions, chopped

1 rib celery, chopped fine

3 cloves garlic, minced

2 tablespoons corn or canola oil

1 teaspoon ground cumin

1 tablespoon chili powder, or to taste

1/2 teaspoon crushed red pepper, or to taste

Makes 8 to 10 servings.

Doing this in a two-day operation makes sense. The recipe is large enough for a crowd, and is easily doubled.

Place turkey in large kettle with water to cover. Add carrot, celery cut in chunks, whole onion, bay leaf, 1 teaspoon salt, and 1/4 teaspoon pepper. Bring to a boil, skimming solids as they rise to the top; cover and simmer 45 minutes, or until turkey is tender. Remove from broth and cool. Discard bay leaf. While turkey is cooling, boil broth rapidly, uncovered, to reduce to 3 cups. Cut turkey meat off bones in cubes or shred it and discard bones, fat, skin, and cartilage.

Meanwhile, cook beans. Cover with water and soak overnight. Pour off water, add fresh water, and cook until tender but not mushy, 1 to 1 1/2 hours. Add remaining 2 teaspoons salt.

To assemble chili, sauté bell pepper, chopped onion, celery, and garlic in oil in large kettle until onion is tender but not browned. Add cumin, chili powder, crushed red pepper, turkey broth, and meat. Ladle beans from liquid with slotted spoon and add to chili. Bring to a boil, partially cover, and simmer 30 minutes to blend flavors. Add bean liquid if needed. Leftovers can be frozen and reheated.

CLASSIC TEXAS BEANS

Beans are a side dish to chili made without beans; barbecue; or sausages in Texas and a condiment in a beef-eating menu, so beans are generally flavored very simply.

1 pound pinto beans (see Note below)
Water
1/4 pound salt pork, cut almost to rind in slices
Salt to taste
Chopped onion and chiles, optional

Makes 10 side-dish servings or 8 main-dish servings.

Wash beans and soak overnight in water to cover. Drain; add fresh water and the pork. Bring to a boil and simmer 45 minutes, adding hot water as needed to keep moist. Add 1½ teaspoons salt and simmer 30 minutes longer, or until tender. Ladle from broth and serve as a side dish to chili or barbecue, or mash and use as base for Frijoles Refritos (recipe follows). Garnish with chopped onion and chiles, if desired.

Note: Red or pink beans can be used if pinto beans are hard to get.

FRIJOLES REFRITOS

    A *Texan, and most Californians, Arizonans, and New Mexicans, wouldn't think of barbecue without refried beans, the American translation of a major Mexican food. Ordinarily Frijoles are loaded with lard but this defatted version tastes mighty good when the barbecue is good.*

Classic Texas Beans (page 217)

2 tablespoons vegetable or corn oil

Salt and pepper to taste

½ cup shredded Monterey Jack or mozzarella cheese

Makes 6 to 8 servings.

Ladle beans from liquid with slotted spoon and place in large deep skillet with oil. Mash beans with potato masher or back of a heavy spoon. Cook and stir until thickened, adding bean liquid to keep moist, but beans should not be runny. Place on warm platter or individual plates and sprinkle with salt and pepper to taste and cheese. Beans should be hot enough to melt cheese.

MAQUE CHOUX

    Louisiana Cajuns are legendary party givers. This summer vegetable stew is served with mountains of steamed crabs or crawfish or other Cajun delectables piled on tables covered with butcher paper.

6 slices bacon

1 medium onion, chopped

½ small green bell pepper, chopped

4 Creole tomatoes, peeled and chopped,
      or 1 (14½-ounce) can tomatoes

10 ears fresh young corn, kernels cut off cobs

1 teaspoon freshly ground pepper

1 teaspoon salt

Makes 6 to 8 servings.

In large saucepan, sauté bacon until crisp. Remove bacon, drain, and crumble. Cook onion and bell pepper in bacon drippings until tender but not browned. Add tomatoes and simmer uncovered 15 to 20 minutes, stirring often. Add corn and pepper to taste. Simmer 10 minutes. Stir in salt and sprinkle with bacon. Serve hot with steamed, barbecued, or grilled fish.

CALIFORNIA CHILI BEANS

Californians prefer pink beans to red or pinto beans and cook them with water, not tomatoes. The beans are seasoned lightly to modify the heat of spicy salsa or barbecued meat.

1 pound dried pink, pinto, or red kidney beans

Salt to taste

2 ounces salt pork, diced

1 large onion, diced

2 cloves garlic, minced

1 cup water, or 1 (8-ounce) can tomato sauce

1/2 teaspoon ground cumin

1 teaspoon chili powder, or to taste

Makes 10 to 12 side-dish servings, 6 to 8 as a main dish.

Soak beans overnight in water to cover generously. Drain. Place in a large saucepan or kettle, add fresh water, and bring to a boil. Turn heat low and simmer until beans are tender but not mushy, 1½ to 2 hours. Check often and add boiling water to keep beans barely covered with water but not soupy. When almost tender, add 1 teaspoon salt. Meanwhile, in skillet, fry out salt pork. Add onion and garlic and cook until tender but not browned. Add water or tomato sauce, cumin, and chili powder. Simmer 10 minutes to blend flavors, then stir mixture into beans. Cover and simmer 20 minutes. Taste and add more salt, if needed. Serve as a side dish to barbecued beef, pork, or turkey or as a main dish with hot tortillas or cornbread.

Texas Chili Beans: Follow recipe for California Chili Beans, using pinto beans. Increase cumin to 1 teaspoon and chili powder to 3 or 4 teaspoons.

HEARTS OF PALM

In the Florida piney woods, this is called swamp cabbage. Sliced fresh hearts of palm, bacon, cream, and seasoning make up the classic recipe. I add fresh white cabbage to canned hearts of palm to produce a semblance of the old-time dish. It can be served either as a side dish or a main dish.

1/4 pound bacon or salt pork, diced

1/2 pound tender young cabbage, coarsely shredded

2 (8-ounce) cans hearts of palm, well drained

1/2 cup cream

Salt and freshly ground pepper to taste

1 pint shelled oysters (optional)

Makes 4 to 8 servings.

Fry out bacon or salt pork, add cabbage, and cook slowly until crisp-tender. Slice hearts of palm and add to cabbage. Bring to a boil in juices that are released from the vegetables. Add cream and simmer 2 or 3 minutes. Oysters can be added at this point and cooked just until the edges curl. Serve hot with barbecued pork, chicken, or fried fish.

GO-ALONGS

If you have skillets and saucepans for a grill, almost any vegetable or side dish that you serve indoors is possible with barbecue, but the popular accompaniments are grilled directly over the fire—grill-roasted corn, potatoes, or onions. The Clewiston barbecue in Florida shows how elaborate a simple barbecue can be. Clewiston lies on Lake Okeechobee, within a few miles of thousands of acres of winter vegetables. At a chicken barbecue, every vegetable available is served. Great kettles of water boil on the grill, ready to cook fresh sweet corn. One man assembles enormous platters of crisp vegetables—radishes, celery, carrots, cauliflower, scallions, and winter tomatoes—to be dipped in a zesty sauce. Another makes huge bowls of coleslaw, using crates of new cabbage, scallions, and carrots.

Anything fresh and in season goes with barbecue. Those with summer gardens have a cornucopia of good things to serve with barbecue. Skewering enables you to grill zucchini, eggplant, and sweet peppers. And the best of all side dishes are coleslaw, mammoth salads of garden greens, and sliced tomatoes still warm from the summer sun.

Other accompaniments here include two kinds of hushpuppies, obligatory with ribs as well as fried fish in some parts of the country; chile cornbread, served with grilled steak in the Southwest and California; and green corn tamale, a summer favorite of Californians.

SKEWERED VEGETABLES

Eggplant, cut-up onions, zucchini, sweet peppers, and summer squash speared on skewers are ideal go-alongs to barbecued meats in late summer when the garden is at its peak.

Cut eggplant in large cubes or chunks or halve eggplants lengthwise to spear on skewers. The peel helps hold the vegetable secure on the skewer. Treat other vegetables simply; use good-size chunks of zucchini or other squash, peppers, and onions so they don't break off the skewers.

Brush the vegetables once or twice with the barbecue sauce being used for the meat or use a lightly herbed salad dressing or oil on the vegetables to prevent drying out. Since vegetables are being cooked with limited moistening, allow a longer cooking time if you insist on tenderness. Many barbecue fans like their squash still crunchy and eggplant before it is cooked to mush.

SPINACH AND TOMATOES

1 (12-ounce) package fresh spinach or 1 pound
   leaf spinach
2 tablespoons mayonnaise
Grated Parmesan cheese
1 tablespoon minced onion
Salt and freshly ground pepper
3 large tomatoes
Buttered bread crumbs

Makes 6 servings.

Wash spinach and cook in the water that clings to it until just tender, 3 to 4 minutes. Drain spinach well and chop fine. Mix spinach, mayonnaise, 2 tablespoons Parmesan cheese, onion, and salt and pepper to taste. Cut tomatoes in half crosswise. Place cut side up in a well-buttered skillet with heat-resistant handle or in a disposable foil pan. Spoon spinach mixture onto tomatoes; sprinkle with bread crumbs and more cheese. Place at edge of grill and heat thoroughly—about 30 minutes on an open grill, 15 to 20 minutes on a covered grill.

BABA GHANOUJ

This Middle Eastern spread is especially suitable for a barbecue appetizer, since charcoal roasting the eggplant gives it authentic flavor. Roast and chill the eggplant the day before you plan to serve it, or serve it slightly warm.

1 large eggplant

Juice of 1 lemon

1 clove garlic, minced

Salt

1 tablespoon minced flat-leaf parsley

1 tablespoon olive oil

Pita bread, cut in quarters

Makes 4 to 6 appetizer servings.

Spear eggplant on a sturdy skewer or fork and grill 4 to 5 inches above hot coals until soft, about 25 minutes. Turn as needed to cook evenly. (Eggplant can be grilled over a gas flame or roasted in a moderate oven until soft, but the flavor will not have the traditional smoky tang.) Let eggplant cool until you can handle it.

Carefully peel and discard skin. Some of the pulp will stick to the skin, so scrape it off with a spoon. Place eggplant pulp in a bowl and squeeze lemon juice on it. Beat in garlic and salt to taste. Pile into a small serving dish. Sprinkle with parsley and drizzle with olive oil. Cover and chill until ready to serve. Surround with pita bread to be spread with baba ghanouj.

SKEWERED SUMMER SQUASH

The woodsy smoke brings out the best of summer squash flavor when it is brushed generously with olive oil and touched with garlic.

2 small yellow summer squash per person
2 cloves garlic, minced
½ cup olive oil
Salt and freshly ground pepper
Butter

Wash squash. Thread diagonally on skewers. (Squash can be cut if large, but they tend to cook to mush if the seedy sides are exposed.) Add garlic to oil and heat slightly.

Brush squash with oil and grill over moderately hot coals at edge of grill 15 to 20 minutes, turning and basting with garlic oil as needed. Serve with salt, a generous grind of pepper, and melted butter.

PEPPERED SUMMER SQUASH

2 tablespoons olive oil
2 teaspoons red wine vinegar
½ teaspoon freshly ground pepper
4 medium yellow summer squash
Butter, salt, and additional pepper

Makes 4 servings.

Pour oil and vinegar into a shallow bowl or pie plate, grind in ½ teaspoon pepper, then beat with a fork. Wash squash, split lengthwise, place in dressing bowl, and turn in the peppery dressing.

Grill cut side down over hot coals about 5 minutes or until tinged with brown. Turn, brush with remaining sauce, and grill until browned on skin side. Brush again with sauce and move to edge of grill to keep warm or serve at once with butter, salt, and more pepper. Total cooking time will be about 10 minutes.

ROASTED ONIONS

Sweet onions such as Vidalia onions from Georgia, Walla Walla onions from Washington State, Maui onions from Hawaii, and Hidalgo onions from Texas are wonderful cooked this way.

1 medium to large onion per person
Butter, salt, and freshly ground pepper

Pull off any loose skin from each onion but do not peel or cut. Wrap each onion in foil and seal tightly closed. Place over hot fire, 4 to 5 inches above coals. Roast until onions are tender when pierced with a fork, about 1 hour for medium to medium-large onions. Serve each person an onion still in its foil wrapper (it's not fair for the host or hostess to have to peel onions). Each person peels off the foil, splits or peels the onion, then butters it liberally and sprinkles it with salt and pepper.

ZUCCHINI OR EGGPLANT PARMESAN

1½ pounds zucchini or eggplant
2 tablespoons vinegar
1 clove garlic, minced
½ teaspoon salt
½ teaspoon freshly ground pepper
½ teaspoon paprika
⅓ cup olive oil
3 tablespoons grated Parmesan cheese

Makes 6 servings.

Scrub zucchini and cut in half lengthwise, or cut unpeeled eggplant in thick slices. Beat together vinegar, garlic, salt, pepper, paprika, and oil.

Place zucchini (cut side down) or eggplant pieces on grill 4 to 5 inches above hot coals, brush with oil mixture, and grill until tender, about 15 minutes, turning and basting as needed to cook evenly. Turn, brush again with dressing, and sprinkle with cheese. Grill until cheese is lightly toasted. Serve hot.

EGGPLANT STACKS

Each person is served a short stack of vegetables—eggplant is the base, topped with tomato and onion. The eggplant and tomato are tender and the flavors blended. The onion is still crispy. Cheese is softened atop the vegetable clumps for a saucelike topping.

1 clove garlic, peeled and split

1/2 cup olive oil

2 tablespoons dry red wine or wine vinegar

1 eggplant, about 1 1/2 pounds

2 tomatoes, about 1/3 pound each

1 small onion

3 slices Muenster or Monterey Jack cheese

Makes 6 servings.

Cook garlic in oil until it is golden. Remove garlic and cool oil slightly. Beat in wine or vinegar. Wash eggplant, but do not peel. Wash tomatoes and peel onion. Cut eggplant crosswise into thick slices. Slice tomatoes, making as many tomato as eggplant slices. Slice onion. Brush both sides of eggplant slices with the garlic oil. Place eggplant slices at edge of grill. Top each with a tomato slice, then an onion slice. Brush again with garlic oil dressing. Grill until heated through and tomatoes begin to moisten eggplant. Move eggplant stacks about with a spatula now and then to make sure they don't stick. Top with a half slice cheese each and grill until cheese is soft. Remove to platter and serve hot.

ONION STEAKS

Large sweet Spanish onions, the American-grown relative of the Bermuda onion and sometimes labeled Bermuda onions in markets, are ideal for this. The "steaks" will be the size of your outstretched palm.

2 large sweet Spanish onions, about 12 ounces each

Milk (fresh whole, skim, or buttermilk)

1 bay leaf, crumbled

About ½ cup flour

2 tablespoons oil

2 tablespoons butter

Salt and freshly ground pepper

Makes 6 servings.

Cut three ½-inch slices from the widest part of each onion, saving ends for other uses. Peel onion slices. Arrange in a shallow dish and almost cover with milk. Crumble bay leaf over onions and milk. Cover and refrigerate 3 to 4 hours, carefully turning onions once or twice. About 20 minutes before serving, remove onions from milk, handling carefully with a spatula so slices don't separate. (Milk can be saved for use in soup, sauces, or gravies.) Coat onions with flour. In a heavy skillet heat oil and butter over moderate heat at edge of grill. Cook onion "steaks" in hot fat until golden; turn and brown the other side. Season well with salt and pepper.

SWEET–SOUR ONIONS

This savory side dish to chicken, ribs, or burgers can be served hot, chilled, or at room temperature, a boon to the barbecue cook who can't coordinate fire and meat to a certain time.

4 medium onions, 1¼ pounds
1 tablespoon cider vinegar
1 tablespoon sugar
2 tablespoons catsup
½ teaspoon salt, or to taste
1 cup water
1½ teaspoons cornstarch

Makes 4 to 6 servings.

Peel and slice onions about ½ inch thick. Place in a 1½-quart stainless-steel or enamelware saucepan. Add vinegar, sugar, catsup, salt, and water. Water should about half cover onions. Cover pan and bring to a boil, turn heat low and simmer 20 minutes or until onions are crisp-tender. Add a small amount of water to cornstarch and stir to a smooth paste. Stir into onion mixture, cooking and stirring until smooth and translucent. Remove from heat. Serve at once, cool to room temperature, or chill before serving.

CREAMY GRITS

Don't feel ignorant if you aren't quite sure what grits is; just enjoy the discovery, as did my young friend who was busily cooking "big hominy," the swollen corn kernels that can be ground to make grits. Hominy grits comes in a package or bag and looks like fine chips of rice or dry corn. Properly cooked, grits makes a wonderful creamy-textured accompaniment to barbecued pork or game.

3 cups water

½ teaspoon salt, or to taste

¾ cup grits (not quick-cooking)

½ cup cold milk

2 tablespoons butter

Makes 4 servings.

In a covered saucepan or top of a double boiler bring water to a boil. Add salt and stir in grits. Move saucepan to low heat or place double boiler top over boiling water. Cover and cook 15 minutes, stirring once or twice to keep smooth. Stir in cold milk, cover, and cook 5 minutes longer over direct heat or 10 to 15 minutes longer in double boiler. Stir in butter, cover, and cook 2 or 3 minutes longer. Serve hot with additional butter at table.

GARLIC GRITS ON THE GRILL

A *shortcut version of this dish, using packaged garlic cheese spread, is served by camp cooks with fried fish. I like this creamier grits dish, flavored with sharp Cheddar and a fresh clove garlic, with pork or game, as well as fish.*

3½ cups water

½ teaspoon salt, or to taste

¾ cup grits (not quick-cooking)

2 tablespoons butter

1 egg

2 ounces Cheddar cheese, coarsely shredded (to make
    ¼ cup)

1 clove garlic, peeled, smashed, and minced

Makes 4

servings.

In a heavy saucepan with tight-fitting cover bring water to a boil. Add salt and stir in grits. Cover and move pan to low heat. Cook, stirring now and then, until smooth and cooked to the consistency of very thick cream, about 15 minutes. Stir in butter and cook and stir until melted. In a small bowl beat egg and stir in a spoonful of the hot grits mixture. Stir the egg into the bubbling grits, cooking and stirring until well mixed. Stir in cheese and garlic, and cook and stir until cheese is melted into grits. Serve hot with additional butter.

GREEN CORN TAMALE

The farmland created by a flood control dam on the Los Angeles River about 15 miles west of city hall was planted in sweet corn when we lived nearby. Most of the crop was sold from streetside stands. Our Sunday afternoon ritual was to drive to Marie's Corn and wait in line for the freshly picked corn to be brought to the shed. Marie, a woman of vast wealth, it was rumored, operated the sales booth. Fieldmen harvested the corn and brought it to the stand minutes later. Marie and her daughter, their hands protected by heavy gloves, would pull a swath of shucks off each ear to check for kernel size and pest damage, then ask if you wanted small, medium, or large kernels. We chose small to grill in the husks and were mystified by our Mexican neighbors, who preferred large kernels.

One Sunday, when I asked a man why he picked the larger, starchier kernels, he replied, "Green tamale." He explained how he made it, but only after several trials and some coaching by a friend who had inherited a recipe from an early governor of California did I master green corn tamale. This version works even in the oven of my New York apartment. The secret is to get a pasty dough that is not runny. I serve green corn tamale with steak, barbecued or broiled chicken, pork, or lamb, as well as with Mexican-style foods. The sweetness imparted by the corn husks produces a flavor unmatched by any other corn preparation that I've had.

The term green corn refers to fresh corn in green shucks, as compared to dried corn used for tortilla meal and the dried husks used for tamales when green corn is not in season.

10 ears mature green corn

1 teaspoon salt

1/2 stick (1/4 cup) butter, melted

1 cup corn meal, or as needed

1/2 pound Cheddar or Monterey Jack cheese, coarsely
    shredded

1 (4-ounce) can whole green chiles, drained and cut in
    strips

Makes 6 to 8 servings.

Shuck corn, reserving a dozen or so large husks. Wash husks and lay flat in a dish of water to keep moist. Remove silks from corn and cut corn off cobs deeply. A corn cutter can be used, but I stand each ear upright in a large shallow bowl and cut from top to bottom with a sharp knife. The corn can be chopped in a food processor, blender, or food grinder—or with a *metate*, a three-legged grinding stone that still is in use in the Southwest and Mexico. Grind the corn until it is doughy, though small pieces of fiber will remain. Season with salt and butter. Stir in enough corn meal to form a dough that holds its shape when pressed in the hand. If too crumbly, add more butter or a little water.

Line a well-greased 2-quart baking dish with corn husks, letting ends extend above rim. Spread a thin layer of the corn mixture over husks to anchor them. Sprinkle cheese over corn, then distribute chiles evenly in baking dish. Cover with remaining corn dough, fold husks over tamale, and press into top. Press additional husks into tamale. Preheat oven to 350 degrees and bake until firm but not dry, about 45 minutes. If top dries out before tamale is set, cover with foil. Serve hot with barbecued meat or beans.

GRILLED CORN

Corn cooked this way in view of the corn row makes every minute of time and energy put into a garden worth it. Harvest it just before you start the fire, and give the corn a half-hour soak in ice water to help it stay moist and tender while grilling it. It's hard to say how many eight ears of corn will serve. I've seen a mere boy eat four ears of corn cooked this way.

8 ears corn

Ice water in a clean pail

Butter, salt, and freshly ground pepper

Makes about 4 servings.

Pull back husks from corn and carefully remove silks. Push husks back in place and, if necessary, tie to hold husks firmly around corn. Soak corn in ice water at least 30 minutes.

Shake off excess water and place corn 4 to 6 inches above hot coals. Cook and turn to cook evenly until a test kernel spurts out juice when pierced with a knife point. This takes about 20 minutes. Serve immediately with butter, salt, and pepper.

CORN FOR A CROWD

A *separate grill for cooking corn when you are catering to a crowd simplifies traffic. The pot of water can be balanced in the center of the grill. Corn cooking works best as a team effort—one crew to husk and clean the corn, another to watch the boiling pot and cook the corn, and another to serve and clean up.*

You'll need a huge kettle. Fill it about 2/3 full and add 1 tablespoon sugar for each gallon of water (salt toughens corn; sugar accentuates the sweetness). Bring water to a boil. On a charcoal fire this may take up to a half hour. Add the freshly shucked corn an ear at a time, cover the pot, and bring again to a boil. Spread fire so heat dies to almost nothing and water ceases to boil. Let corn stand 6 to 7 minutes. Serve with butter, salt, and pepper.

Note: When passing corn outdoors, wrapping a half-dozen or so ears in a napkin or clean kitchen towel in a basket keeps it hot longer. The corn left in a large pot of hot water will hold for 20 or 30 minutes if the water is not allowed to boil again.

OLD WORLD RED CABBAGE

Red cabbage is a rich complement to game birds and meats, and can be cooked in a deep skillet on the grill. We cook it in the kitchen and reheat it on the grill. Bits of fat trimmed from pheasant or poultry are good in red cabbage, but with venison use salt pork or ham bits, which has the fat trimmed away and discarded.

2 tablespoons rendered pheasant or poultry fat, vegetable oil, butter, or ¼ pound salt pork or ham fat, diced

Makes 4 generous servings.

1 medium onion, chopped

1 medium carrot, peeled and sliced

1 clove garlic, minced

1½ pounds red cabbage, shredded coarsely

1 large apple, peeled and chopped, or 1 cup applesauce

1 tablespoon rice or balsamic vinegar

1 cup robust red wine

2 cups beef broth

¼ teaspoon ground allspice

⅛ teaspoon ground nutmeg

⅛ teaspoon freshly ground pepper

Salt

Heat fat in large saucepan or Dutch oven. Add onion and carrot and stir until onion is translucent. Add garlic, cabbage, and apple. Stir to mix well. Add vinegar, wine, beef broth, allspice, nutmeg, and pepper. Cook and stir uncovered until boiling. Cover and simmer 45 minutes to 1 hour, stirring now and then. Uncover and simmer until cabbage is tender and most of juice is evaporated. Salt to taste and serve hot with poultry, game, or pork.

WILD OR BROWN RICE

Pheasant bits are a luxurious extra with rice, but any meaty broth is good. Cook this in a saucepan at the side of the grill or bring it from the kitchen.

Backs, wing tips, and trimmings from 2 pheasants

1 onion, peeled and studded with 3 whole cloves

1 large carrot, peeled and cut in chunks

3 to 4 cups water

2 teaspoons salt, or to taste

⅛ teaspoon pepper

1 bay leaf

1 teaspoon whole allspice

Dried or fresh peel of 1 orange

1 cup wild or brown rice, or mixture

Makes 4 to 6 servings.

Combine pheasant pieces, onion, carrot, and water to cover in large saucepan. Add 1½ teaspoons salt, the pepper, bay leaf, allspice, and orange peel. Bring to a boil, skimming solids that rise to top. Cover and simmer 45 minutes. Strain, pick meat bits off bones, and return to broth.

Bring 2½ cups broth to a boil in saucepan. Add rice and remaining ½ teaspoon salt. Cover and simmer 50 minutes, until rice is tender and liquid absorbed. Serve hot.

CHILE CORNBREAD

Quite typical of Texas and California, this cornbread must be baked in an oven. Serve it with a thick steak, cooked juicy rare, and an enormous bowl of green salad—a favorite summer evening combination in Hollywood. The cornbread is brought piping hot from the kitchen.

1/4 cup oil or bacon drippings

1 1/2 cups corn meal

1/2 cup flour

4 teaspoons baking powder

1/2 teaspoon salt

1 cup milk

2 eggs

1 (16-ounce) can cream-style corn

1 (4-ounce) can whole green chiles, seeded and cut
    in strips

1/4 pound Cheddar cheese, coarsely shredded

Makes
10 to 12
servings.

Preheat oven to 425 degrees. Add oil or drippings to a 9-inch skillet and while preheating the oven place pan in it to heat. A 9-inch-square baking pan also can be used.

In a bowl mix corn meal, flour, baking powder, and salt. Stir in milk and eggs. Remove pan from oven and pour oil into batter, leaving a heavy film of oil in pan. Mix batter well and pour half of it into hot pan. Spoon corn over batter, then arrange chiles over corn and sprinkle with cheese. Cover with remaining batter. Bake 25 minutes or until golden and done through. Center will be moist and custardy. Cut in wedges or squares and serve with butter.

CHILE–CORN CAKES

Chile-cheese cornbread is traditional with grilled steak in the Southwest. This version is crusty on the outside, soft as spoon bread in the interior, so it is eaten with a fork. A well-seasoned small black-iron skillet cooks it perfectly.

1/2 cup water-ground white corn meal
1/2 teaspoon salt
1 cup boiling water
1/4 cup cold milk
2 to 3 tablespoons oil
1/4 cup corn cut off the cob
1 1/2 ounces sharp Cheddar cheese, coarsely shredded
　　(to make 1/3 cup)
1/2 to 1 canned green chiles, cut in strips

Makes 4 servings.

In a small bowl combine corn meal and salt. Add boiling water and stir until smooth. Let stand 15 to 20 minutes. Batter will thicken. Stir in cold milk to thin slightly.

Heat a 7-inch cast-iron or other heavy skillet thoroughly. Add 1 tablespoon oil and heat until sizzling. Add half the batter and tilt pan to let batter cover bottom of pan. Place pan over moderate heat and sprinkle corn cake with half the corn and cheese and arrange half the chiles on corn cake. Cook about 3 minutes, until underside is browned and firm. Carefully lift 1 edge of corn cake and fold over other half to form a half-moon shape. Cook 10 minutes longer, turning once or twice to brown well on both sides. Add oil to skillet, if needed. Remove corn cake to hot platter and keep warm. Cook remaining corn cake, adding more oil to skillet. Serve hot, cutting each half-moon in 2 portions. This crispy cornbread needs no additional butter.

TALLAHASSEE HUSHPUPPIES

Camp cooks, the story goes, fried corn cakes for the dogs, along with fish for the people, and tossed the cornbread to the dogs, saying, "Hush, puppy." A cook thought to taste a crispy nugget, and an American folk food was born. Hushpuppies go with fish, but are a barbecue regular, too.

1¾ cups white corn meal, preferably water-ground

¼ cup flour

2 teaspoons baking powder

1 teaspoon baking soda

1 teaspoon salt

½ teaspoon freshly ground pepper, or more to taste

1 large onion, finely chopped

1½ cups buttermilk or beer

2 eggs

Oil for frying

Makes 24 flat hush-puppies, 6 to 8 servings.

In a bowl combine corn meal, flour, baking powder, baking soda, salt, pepper, and onion. Stir in buttermilk or beer and eggs until well mixed. Hushpuppies customarily are fried in drippings from fried fish. You need ½ inch hot fish drippings or oil. Drop batter into hot oil by tablespoonfuls and cook until browned and puffed. Turn and brown the other side. Remove from fat and drain on paper towels. Continue cooking until all batter is used. Serve hot with fried fish, barbecue, or vegetables.

Note: These are light puffy corn cakes, not the hard doughy balls that are served as hushpuppies in most commercial places.

BARBECUED BREAD

Anybody who ate through the fifties and sixties knows garlic bread and bread spread with butter or olive oil, sprinkled with herbs complementary to the meat, and grilled over the fire as meat is finished.

Barbecued bread is old stuff to lots of outdoor chefs. Simply brush thick slices of French, Italian, or rye bread with a thin barbecue sauce, invert it over dying coals, and roast it lightly. This was designed to go with the meal, but hungry kibitzers often wolf it down before the chef is ready to serve the main dish of the evening.

BISHOP'S HUSHPUPPIES

Bishop, a maintenance man at Texas A & M, has become a minor celebrity for his hushpuppies, spiced with three peppers and other seasonings. He and fellow workers periodically invite friends for a feast of catfish, beans, coleslaw, other Texas specialties, and the hushpuppies. Latecomers are in danger of missing out on the hushpuppies, so this is one party at which guests arrive on time.

1 cup each water-ground white corn meal and flour

2 teaspoons baking powder

1 teaspoon baking soda

1 teaspoon salt

1/2 teaspoon freshly ground pepper

1 medium yellow onion, finely chopped

4 scallions, including tops, finely chopped

1 or 2 jalapeño peppers, seeds removed, finely chopped

1 roasted and peeled fresh or canned sweet red pepper, chopped

1½ cups buttermilk

2 eggs

Oil for frying

Makes about 24 flat hush-puppies, 6 to 8 servings.

In a large bowl combine corn meal, flour, baking powder, baking soda, salt, black pepper, onion, scallions, jalapeño, and red pepper. In another bowl, stir together buttermilk and eggs until well mixed. Stir into dry ingredients.

Pour 1/2 inch oil into a large heavy skillet and heat until almost sizzling. Drop batter into hot oil by tablespoonfuls and cook over moderate heat until browned and puffy; turn and brown other side. Remove from fat with a slotted spoon and drain on paper towels. Keep hot while frying remaining hushpuppies. Add more oil to skillet as needed to maintain 1/2-inch depth. Serve hushpuppies hot. They're especially good with fried catfish, barbecued pork, or vegetables.

VEGETABLE–BACON KEBABS

Cubes of eggplant, partially cooked carrot chunks, and mushrooms steamed slightly to prevent splitting can join these vegetables to grill on skewers.

2 yellow summer squash, about ¾ pound

2 zucchini, about ¾ pound in all

4 medium onions

4 large sweet red peppers

½ cup oil

¼ cup cider or wine vinegar

2 tablespoons minced fresh or 1 teaspoon dried basil

1 tablespoon minced fresh or ½ teaspoon dried thyme

2 tablespoons minced fresh parsley

6 to 8 slices bacon, cut in 1-inch pieces

Makes 6 to 8 servings.

Wash squash and zucchini and cut in 1-inch slices. Peel onions and cut into 4 wedges each. Seed and core peppers and cut in 12 squares each. Place vegetables in a plastic bag. Mix oil, vinegar, and herbs. Pour into bag, close bag tightly, and turn to coat vegetables well. Marinate at room temperature at least 2 hours. Thread vegetables on skewers, alternating types and placing a bacon piece between vegetables at intervals.

Grill 4 to 6 inches over hot coals 10 to 15 minutes, turning to cook evenly and brushing with marinade now and then.

COUNTRY-FRIED POTATOES

This simple old-fashioned food goes with almost any barbecued meat, and can be prepared at the edge of the grill with no special planning at all. I like the potatoes best when they are sliced and cooked unpeeled, but do as you please.

6 large thin-skinned potatoes, about 2 pounds

1 medium yellow onion, 2 to 3 ounces

3 tablespoons bacon or other meat drippings or oil

1/2 teaspoon salt

Freshly ground pepper

Makes 4 servings.

Peel potatoes or scour well with a brush under running water. Cut in 1/4-inch slices. Peel and slice onion. In a large skillet heat drippings or oil. Add potatoes and onion and stir with a spatula to mix well. Cover and move to moderate heat. Cook about 10 minutes, watching to make sure potato and onion don't burn. Uncover, season with salt and pepper, and cook 10 to 15 minutes longer, until potatoes are tender and lightly browned.

Note: For variety, chopped green pepper, fresh green peas, snow peas, or thinly sliced carrot can be added to potatoes.

GRILLED POTATOES WITH CHEESE

4 baking potatoes, about 6 ounces each

1 large onion, sliced

1/4 cup grated Parmesan cheese

4 teaspoons butter

Salt and freshly ground pepper

Makes 4 large servings.

Peel potatoes and slice crosswise. Tear 4 squares heavy-duty foil and butter 1 side heavily. On buttered side of each square of foil pile a sliced potato, some onion, cheese, 1 teaspoon butter, and salt and pepper to taste. If potatoes look dry, add a tablespoon cream. Wrap foil packets loosely around potatoes and seal with a double fold. Grill over hot coals until potatoes are tender, about 30 minutes, turning packets to cook evenly. Turn out a packetful of potato onto each dinner plate.

GRILL–ROASTED WHITE OR SWEET POTATOES

1 potato per person

Oil (optional)

Butter, salt, and freshly ground pepper

Scrub potatoes. If soft skin is desired, oil skins well. For crisp skins, do not oil. Place potatoes over medium heat on grill and cook, turning every 15 minutes or so, until tender when pierced with a fork. Russets or other large white potatoes usually require 1 to 1½ hours; small potatoes, 45 minutes to 1 hour; and sweet potatoes, 45 minutes to 1 hour. Serve hot, slit skin in a cross and press potato to push up flesh through skin. Serve with lots of butter, salt, and pepper.

MY GRANDMOTHER'S POTATO SALAD

This basic potato salad is first-rate with barbecue, but you could add such things as sliced olives or pickle relish.

2½ pounds waxy potatoes, California potatoes, or other thin-skinned new potatoes

2 eggs

1 teaspoon Dijon-style mustard

2 tablespoons sherry, balsamic, or cider vinegar

3 tablespoons olive oil

2 large scallions with tops, thinly sliced

2 ribs celery, diced

½ cup mayonnaise

1 teaspoon celery seed

Salt and freshly ground pepper

Makes 6 to 8 servings.

Scrub potatoes and place in a large saucepan with enough water to barely cover. Cover pan, bring to a boil, and boil 10 minutes. Meanwhile, rinse eggs in hot water to warm them slightly to prevent cracking. Add eggs to potatoes and continue cooking until potatoes are barely tender. Eggs must cook at least 10 minutes. If potatoes are tender before they have cooked 10 minutes, lift out with slotted spoon. Cool potatoes just enough to handle and cool eggs promptly in cold water. Crack and shell eggs, pulling off membrane with shell. Wrap eggs individually in plastic wrap and refrigerate. Peel potatoes and cube them into a bowl.

In a small bowl stir together mustard and vinegar, then beat in olive oil. Pour over potatoes and toss to coat potatoes well. Cover and refrigerate 2 or 3 hours. To finish salad, add scallions, celery, mayonnaise to moisten, celery seed, and salt and pepper to taste. Toss gently but thoroughly. Turn into serving bowl and tuck crisp greens around the edges. Slice eggs and arrange in circle around outside of potato salad. Cover and refrigerate or serve at once.

BUTTERED POTATOES

A *French family was grilling these richly flavored potatoes on a tiny brazier when we picnicked near Avignon one spring Sunday. The family happily posed for a picture, pushing the smallest child front center to hide the grill and potatoes (the objects that we wanted on film), so we have a smiling little boy in our snapshot and no potatoes. We've grilled potatoes this way many times since.*

4 potatoes, about 4 ounces each	*Makes*
1 stick (½ cup) butter	*4 to 6*
Salt and freshly ground pepper	*servings.*

Peel potatoes, if desired, though I like the peel left on. Cut lengthwise in thick slabs. In a small saucepan melt butter at edge of grill. Brush potatoes with butter and place on grill 4 to 6 inches above hot coals. Grill, turning and basting with butter as needed to cook evenly and prevent flames, until potatoes are golden brown and tender, about 20 minutes' total cooking. Serve hot with remaining or more butter and salt and pepper.

BRANDIED MUSHROOMS

Flambé *these mushrooms for a dramatic accompaniment to a thick steak or burgers.*

½ stick (¼ cup) butter	*Makes*
1 tablespoon minced shallots or scallions	*4 to 6*
10 to 12 ounces fresh mushrooms, cleaned and sliced	*servings.*
Dash salt	
¼ teaspoon freshly ground pepper	
2 tablespoons brandy	
½ cup heavy cream, or ¼ cup beef broth	
or dry red wine	

In a skillet melt butter. Add shallots or scallions and sauté until aroma begins to deepen, 5 to 6 minutes. Add mushrooms and cook briefly, stirring gently once or twice. Add salt and pepper and stir once. Tip skillet so mushrooms and juices slide to one side of pan. Set pan straight and add brandy to dry side of pan. Immediately ignite. Stir in cream, broth, or wine as flame dies. Heat but do not boil. Serve with steak or thick hamburgers.

MUSHROOM WILD RICE

This is very special with beef, chicken, or turkey but some barbecue chefs serve it with anything from hot dogs to lamb.

1 stick (1/2 cup) butter

12 ounces fresh mushrooms, cleaned and sliced

1½ cups wild rice

1½ cups beef broth, or more as needed

1½ cups mixed vegetable juice

Salt and freshly ground pepper

Makes 6 to 8 servings.

In a heavy Dutch oven melt butter. Add mushrooms and sauté until liquid that cooks from mushrooms is evaporated. Add wild rice and sauté, stirring occasionally, until well coated with butter and smelling lightly toasted. Add broth, vegetable juice, and salt and pepper to taste. Bring to a boil, cover, and simmer 1½ hours, stirring now and then. If not ready to serve, add more beef broth, move to edge of grill, or turn oven heat very low and keep warm. The seasonings permeate the rice thoroughly when cooked this way and if made the day before, the dish can be reheated by adding a little hot broth.

FOUR PEPPERS SALAD

Anybody who finds a rainbow assortment of sweet peppers in late summer can serve this glorious salad. Specialty growers in our part of the country supply us and you can grow these fancy peppers from seed, if you are a gardener.

A large handful garden lettuce

1 each sweet green, red, yellow, and purple pepper

1 large scallion, sliced

6 to 8 cherry tomatoes, halved

About 3 tablespoons olive oil

About 1 tablespoon sherry vinegar

Salt and freshly ground pepper

Makes 6 to 8 servings.

Wash greens well, dry thoroughly, and tear into bite-size pieces into a salad bowl lined with paper towels to blot up stray drops of water. Discard towels, dumping greens back into bowl. Remove seeds and ribs from peppers, cut in rings, and arrange in separate piles over greens. Pile green onion in center and arrange tomatoes in another pile. Cover and chill until ready to serve. Bring salad to table before tossing.

Sprinkle with oil to moisten, toss gently, then add vinegar, salt, and pepper and toss lightly. Serve immediately.

ROASTED ORANGE HALVES

2 navel oranges

3 tablespoons melted butter or barbecue sauce

Makes 4 servings.

Place oranges in a large pot with water to cover. Bring to a boil and simmer until oranges are tender enough to be pierced easily with a skewer, about 25 minutes for medium oranges. Drain and cool oranges. Cut crosswise in half. Place skin side down at edge of grill and brush with melted butter or barbecue sauce (such as sauces with Smoky Ginger Duckling, page 105) and heat thoroughly. Brush again with sauce and turn cut side down. Grill until lightly browned and heated through. Serve—skin and all—with pork or poultry.

TEXAS COLESLAW

No salad goes with barbecued ribs as well as coleslaw, and I serve it with almost any barbecue.

1 pound firm white cabbage
1/2 small onion
2 tablespoons sweet pickle relish
1/4 cup mayonnaise, or to taste
Salt to taste

Makes 4 to 6 servings.

Cut cabbage in wedges and cut out core. Peel onion and cut in wedges. Cut cabbage and onion on slicing blade of processor or shred coarsely. In bowl combine with pickle relish and mayonnaise to moisten well. Taste and add salt, if needed. Pickle relish provides enough sweetness for me. If you like sweeter coleslaw, add sugar to taste. Cover coleslaw and refrigerate until ready to serve.

FRESH CUCUMBER RELISH

2 cucumbers
1/2 small onion
1 teaspoon salt
1 tablespoon minced fresh dill, or 1/2 teaspoon dill weed
3 to 4 tablespoons cider vinegar

Makes 2 cups or 6 to 8 relish servings.

If cucumbers are waxed, scour with a brush and tepid suds made with dishwashing liquid detergent; rinse thoroughly and dry. Peel off bands of green skin so that about half the green portion remains to tint relish pale green. In a food processor or on a hand shredder, coarsely shred cucumbers and onion. In an enamelware, stainless-steel, or plastic colander, combine cucumbers, onion, and salt. Let stand in sink 15 minutes. Press out as much liquid as possible. Turn relish into bowl; stir in dill and vinegar. Cover and refrigerate until ready to serve.

EASTERN CAROLINA COLESLAW

Coleslaw with a barbecued pork East of Lexington in North Carolina is white tinged with the green or creamy color of pure shredded cabbage. Go to Lexington and West of there and you'll find the slaw is rosy colored, with a touch of catsup and barbecue sauce.

1 head (1½ pounds) cabbage, finely shredded

3 to 4 green onions, with tops, sliced very thin

1 cup mayonnaise

2 tablespoons sugar

2 tablespoons white or cider vinegar

1 teaspoon celery seed

1 teaspoon salt, or to taste

Makes 8 servings.

Combine cabbage and green onions in large bowl. In small bowl, combine mayonnaise, sugar, vinegar, celery seed, and salt. Pour over slaw and toss lightly. Cover and refrigerate 1 hour or until read to serve.

Lexington-style Coleslaw: Omit green onions, celery seed, and vinegar from Eastern Carolina Coleslaw. Beat 1 tablespoon catsup and 2 tablespoons Lexington Style Barbecue Sauce (page 190) into mayonnaise dressing for slaw.

SANTA MARIA SALSA

This is one version of the Cal-Mex cold tomato relish that goes with barbecue and other foods eaten outdoors and at formal dining tables. It goes with steak, beans, lamb, chicken, or turkey on the barbecue table.

2 (14½-ounce) cans tomatoes, or 3½ cups chopped
    peeled fresh tomatoes
½ cup chopped celery
¾ cup chopped onion
¼ cup chopped green pepper
1½ teaspoons salt
1 teaspoon prepared horseradish
1 tablespoon vinegar
1 tablespoon sugar
1 tablespoon Worcestershire sauce
1 pickled jalapeño, minced, or to taste

Makes about 4 cups.

Finely chop canned tomatoes with scissors and mix with other ingredients. Turn into a bowl or jar, cover tightly, and refrigerate several hours or overnight to blend flavors. Serve at room temperature as a side dish with meats, beans, and barbecue. Any leftovers can be refrigerated for several days.

DESSERTS

Desserts after a barbecue fall into three categories: fresh fruits because they are in season; a dessert prepared on or at the grill; and a dessert brought from the kitchen.

I've had hostess-baked devil's food cake, brownies with ice cream and chocolate sauce, lavish trifles, and angel food cake hollowed out and filled with ice cream. Lime pie is popular in Florida and glazed strawberry pie in California.

A barbecue is one of the few times that I think a flaming dessert is justified. The drama seems somehow appropriate when fireflies flit, locusts and katydids supply the music, and night-blooming blossoms scent the air. Almost any fruit can be glazed in a skillet in butter and sugar, then flamed with a high-proof spirit.

But the only dessert you really need is a

selection of good cheeses and a choice of summer's finest fruits—peaches, plums, Bartlett pears, grapes, cherries, or berries. Bring on the coffee and a good port or dessert madeira—what a way to end the day!

PEACH–BLACKBERRY COMPOTE

Raspberries or blueberries can be used instead of the blackberries, but blackberries seem extra summery and are increasingly available in big city markets.

2 cups water
1 cup sugar
1 vanilla bean
2 teaspoons lemon juice
5 to 6 peaches, peeled and sliced
1½ cups blackberries, washed and drained
1 cup heavy cream

Makes
4 to 6
servings.

In a saucepan combine water and sugar and bring to a boil. Split the vanilla bean, scrape out the seeds, and add remaining bean to syrup. Simmer the syrup 15 minutes, until slightly thickened. Remove from heat and stir in lemon juice. Cool slightly. Add peaches to hot syrup, cover, and chill 2 or 3 hours. Spoon peaches and some of the syrup into each dessert dish. Scatter blackberries over the top and serve with cream.

PEACHES IN PORT

If you tire of fresh juicy peaches during barbecue season, this is a refreshing alternative.

6 peaches
2 tablespoons butter
1 tablespoon sugar, or to taste
¼ cup port

Makes 6
servings.

Peel and slice peaches. (If not using at once, cover with water with juice of half a lemon in it. Just before cooking, drain peaches.) Melt butter in a skillet. Add peaches and sugar; cook and turn until peaches are coated with butter mixture. Add port and cook until sauce takes on a syrupy consistency. Serve warm with ice cream, sour cream, or whipped cream.

PEACHES WITH BUTTERED ALMONDS

This can be cooked in the kitchen and served outdoors or cooked at the edge of the grill.

½ stick (¼ cup) butter

¼ cup sliced almonds

2 tablespoons fine dry bread crumbs

2 tablespoons brown sugar

6 firm-ripe peaches

2 tablespoons water

2 to 3 tablespoons granulated sugar

2 teaspoons lemon juice

Makes 6 servings.

Several hours before serving, in a small skillet melt 2 tablespoons of the butter. Add almonds and bread crumbs and stir over moderate heat until lightly toasted and saturated with butter. Stir in brown sugar. Cool.

About 45 minutes before serving, in an 8- or 9-inch skillet heat remaining butter. Peel and slice peaches into hot butter. Cook a minute or 2 over moderate heat, add water, and sprinkle with sugar and lemon juice. Cook, stirring carefully so as not to break up peaches, just until fruit is tender. Spoon into dessert bowls and sprinkle with almond butter. Serve with cream or ice cream, if desired.

PEARS POACHED IN VANILLA SYRUP

2 cups water

1⅓ cups sugar

2 teaspoons vanilla extract

6 firm-ripe pears

Brandy custard sauce or whipped cream (see Note)

*Makes 6
servings.*

In a wide saucepan combine water and sugar. (The poaching syrup should be at least 2 inches deep; double the syrup ingredients, if necessary.) Bring to a boil, stirring until sugar is dissolved, and turn heat low. Peel pears and cut out blossom ends, but do not core. The core helps pear hold its shape. Carefully place pears in syrup and cook, turning with tongs to coat with syrup, until barely tender, 10 to 15 minutes. Lift from syrup and stand upright in a serving dish. After all pears are cooked, turn heat high and boil down syrup until slightly thickened. Pour over pears. Serve warm or cooled with custard or whipped cream.

Note: Make the sauce for these pears using a favorite recipe for soft custard flavored with Cognac or pear brandy, or by whipping some cream and folding in sugar and brandy to taste.

PIES

Homemade pies are traditional desserts for church benefit barbecues. The women of the church bake them, while their menfolk tend the pig cookers and shred the meat. One sunny October afternoon we stopped at Merritt Chapel Methodist Church near Chapel Hill, North Carolina, to check on the pig cooking, said to be the best church barbecue in the region. Instead, we found Mrs. McGeehee, the cook's wife, toting 16 pies into the church social hall. Her pies were lemon, chocolate cream, apple, and pumpkin. Another churchwoman was baking pecan pies, Mrs. McGeehee told us. Pie bakers generally use time-tested recipes. Summer fruit pies and cobblers take advantage of fresh fruit in season.

BUTTERED PEARS

In New York, the first Bartletts come to market in mid-July, so I can serve them for dessert several times before the barbecuing season fades.

4 large, firm-ripe Bartlett pears

3 tablespoons butter

3 tablespoons brown sugar

Vanilla or butter pecan ice cream

Makes 4
large or
8 small
servings.

Peel and slice pears crosswise, removing cores and stringy fiber at center. In a 9- or 10-inch skillet heat butter and sugar. Add pears and stir gently to coat with butter and sugar. Cook, turning occasionally, until pears are tender but not mushy. Serve warm or reheat to serve. Spoon pears into dessert bowls and top each serving with ice cream.

FLAMING BANANAS

Sliced oranges, peaches, pears, or fresh berries can be flamed as well as bananas. Cook the soft fruit only a minute or two and flame with a matching liqueur or brandy.

6 firm-ripe bananas

½ stick (¼ cup) butter

2 tablespoons brown sugar

2 teaspoons lime juice

2 tablespoons dark rum, warmed

Makes 6 to 8 servings.

Peel bananas and cut into 4 pieces each, first lengthwise, then crosswise. In a skillet melt butter. Add bananas and turn in butter to coat well. Sprinkle with brown sugar and lime juice. Simmer 5 minutes, turning bananas once or twice to cook evenly. Place at edge of grill to keep warm. Just before serving, heat until sizzling and push bananas to side of pan. Pour in rum and ignite immediately at dry side of pan. Serve flaming on dessert plates with ice cream, if desired.

WATERMELONS

Local watermelons are dessert for community barbecues in hot weather. One hint that a barbecue is scheduled, as if roadside signs don't tell you, is a mountain of watermelons in the park or churchyard.

DESSERTS

APPLES BAKED ON A GRILL

Baking apples (Rome Beauty, Jonathan, Greening, or
    Granny Smith)
Butter
Brown sugar or honey
Ground cinnamon
Freshly grated nutmeg
Chopped walnuts

For each person, tear off a square of heavy-duty foil large enough to wrap an apple. Core baking apples. Place an apple on each square of foil and fill core cavity with a pat of butter, a tablespoonful of brown sugar or honey, a sprinkle of cinnamon and pinch of nutmeg, and a few chopped nuts. Pull foil up around apple and twist closed to seal packet.

Cook apples at edge of grill, turning as needed to cook evenly. Apples will be tender in 35 to 45 minutes on a covered grill, in up to 1 hour on a brazier. Unwrap each apple over a dessert bowl and pour juices into bowl with apple. Serve warm with cream or milk, if desired.

TOASTED MARSHMALLOW SUNDAES

This is an adult dessert, so if children come to the barbecue substitute chocolate or butterscotch sauce for the liqueur.

6 dessert glasses of ice cream
Tia Maria or other coffee-flavored liqueur
6 marshmallows

Makes 6 servings.

Place ice cream in glasses on a tray and pour a big spoonful of liqueur over each serving so that it drizzles down slowly. Meanwhile, let each person toast his marshmallow over hot coals until golden and smelling of lightly burnt sugar. Slip marshmallow off the fork onto a dish of ice cream and eat.

ROASTED CHESTNUTS

Roasted chestnuts and crisp fall apples or pears make a splendid dessert for a fall barbecue on a weekend when the sunshine cooperates.

Fresh chestnuts in the shell, 12 per person
Corn or other vegetable oil

Peel a thin strip off the flat side of each chestnut, using a sharp paring knife. Toss chestnuts with oil. Place in a shallow pan, long-handled corn popper, or on a double sheet of heavy-duty foil pierced in several places to allow heat to circulate.

Place on grill about 4 inches above hot coals. Roast until shells pull away from nuts and a nutty aroma fills the air. Cool chestnuts just enough to be handled and let each person shell his or her own. The membrane must be peeled off the nut. Provide plenty of paper napkins for handling the chestnuts and wiping oily fingers.

SHOPPING SOURCES FOR SPECIAL FOODS

Fancy food shops in many cities will order most ingredients a barbecue chef wants. Don't overlook local boutique farmers for farmyard-grown chicken and turkey, domesticated game birds, meat goats, and other different foods. Here are mail-order sources for many foods.

Shippers customarily ship on Mondays, so they want orders by Friday for delivery four to five days later, depending on distance. Meats and birds are vacuum packed, frozen, and shipped in insulated containers with dry ice.

BUFFALO (BISON) MEAT

Rocky Mountain Natural Meats, P.O. Box 16668, Denver, Colorado 80216; (303) 287-7100.

Forbes Buffalo Acres, Rt. 4, Box 5, New Castle, Pennsylvania 16101; (412) 658-4082 or 656-8703.

VENISON

Lucky Star Ranch, Rt. 1, Box 273, Chaumont, New York 13622; (607) 836-4766.

GAME BIRDS (FARM-RAISED)

D'Artagnan, Inc., 399–419 St. Paul Avenue, Jersey City, New Jersey 07306; (800) 327-8246. Wide selection, well-known for magret (duck breast).

Durham Nightbird Game & Poultry, 650 San Mateo Avenue, San Bruno, California, 94066; (415) 873-1940.

Foggy Ridge Game Bird Farm, P.O. Box 88, Thomaston, Maine 04861; (207) 273-2357.

Wild Game, Inc., 2315 West Huron Street, Chicago, Illinois 60612; (312) 278-1661.

Wylie Hill Farm, P.O. Box 35, Craftsbury Common, Vermont 05827; (802) 586-2887.

HERBS, SPICES, SEASONINGS

Aphrodisia, 282 Bleecker Street, New York, New York 10014; (212) 989-6440.

BIBLIOGRAPHY

Colquitt, Harriet Ross, *The Savannah Cook Book*, Colonial Publishers, Charleston, South Carolina, Fifth Edition, 1963.

Cook 'Em Horns, Ex-Students Association, University of Texas, Austin, 1981.

Dyer, Ceil, *The Carter Family Favorites Cookbook*, Delacorte Press, New York, New York, 1977.

Eckhardt, Linda West, *The Only Texas Cookbook*, Texas Monthly Press, Austin, Texas, 1981.

Egerton, John, *Southern Food*, Alfred A. Knopf, Inc., New York, New York, 1987.

Gabilondo, Aida, *Mexican Family Cooking*, Ballantine Books, New York, New York, 1986.

Glenn, Camille, *The Heritage of Southern Cooking*, Workman Publishing, New York, New York, 1986.

Hooker, Richard J., *Food and Drink in America*, The Bobbs-Merrill Co., Indianapolis, Indiana, 1981.

Jones, Evan, *American Food, The Gastronomic Story*, E. P. Dutton, New York, New York, 1975.

Madigan, Meg, *Political Potluck*, Peninsular Publishing Co., Tallahassee, Florida, 1959.

Marshall, Lillian Bertram, *Cooking Across the South*, Oxmoor House, Birmingham, Alabama, 1980.

McCulloch-Williams, Martha, *Dishes and Beverages of the Old South*, facsimile of original 1913 edition, with introduction by John Egerton, University of Tennessee Press, Knoxville, 1988.

Wilson, Charles Reagan, and William Ferris, *The Encyclopedia of Southern Culture*, University of North Carolina Press, Chapel Hill, 1989.

A NOTE ABOUT THE AUTHOR

Jeanne Voltz was born in Collinsville, Alabama. She was the food editor at _Woman's Day_ magazine and for many years edited as well the food pages at the Los Angeles _Times_ and the Miami _Herald_. She is the author of several books, including _The California Cookbook_, _The Flavors of the South_, and, with Caroline Stuart, _The Florida Cookbook_. She has won a Tastemaker Award three times and is a six-time winner of the Vesta Award for newspaper food editing and writing. Mrs. Voltz has also won numerous other feature and food writing awards. She lives in Pittsboro, North Carolina, where she is a food consultant, writer, and freelance editor.

A NOTE ON THE TYPE

The text of this book was set in Century Expanded, a type designed in 1894 by Linn Boyd Benton (1844–1933). Benton cut Century Expanded in response to a request by Theodore L. De Vinne for an attractive, easy-to-read typeface to fit the narrow columns of his *Century Magazine*. Early in the 1900s Benton's son, Morris Fuller Benton, updated and improved Century in several versions for his father's American Type Founders Company. Century remains the only American typeface cut before 1900 that is still widely in use today.

Composed by Superior Type, Champaign, Illinois
Printed and bound by The Courier Companies, Inc.,
Westford, Massachusetts
Designed by Stephanie Tevonian
Billboard panorama illustrations by Denis Ziemienski

KNOPF COOKS AMERICAN

The series of cookbooks that celebrates the culinary heritage of America, telling different aspects of our story through recipes interspersed with historical lore, personal reflections, and the recollections of old-timers.

ALREADY PUBLISHED:

Biscuits, Spoonbread, and Sweet Potato Pie by Bill Neal

Hot Links & Country Flavors by Bruce Aidells and Denis Kelly

Barbecued Ribs, Smoked Butts, and Other Great Feeds by Jeanne Voltz

We Called It Macaroni by Nancy Verde Barr

The West Coast Cook Book by Helen Evans Brown

Pleasures of the Good Earth by Edward Giobbi

The Brooklyn Cookbook by Lyn Stallworth and Rod Kennedy, Jr.

Dungeness Crabs and Blackberry Cobblers by Janie Hibler

Preserving Today by Jeanne Lesem

Blue Corn and Chocolate by Elisabeth Rozin

Real Beer & Good Eats by Bruce Aidells and Denis Kelly

The Florida Cookbook by Jeanne Voltz and Caroline Stuart

Jewish Cooking in America by Joan Nathan

Savoring the Seasons of the Northern Heartland by Beth Dooley and Lucia Watson

"Our food tells us where we came from and who we are . . ."

ALSO BY JEANNE VOLTZ

The Florida Cookbook (with Caroline Stuart) (1993)

Community Suppers and Other Glorious Repasts (1987)

Barbecued Ribs and Other Great Feeds (1985)

Gifts from a Country Kitchen (edited) (1984)

An Apple a Day (1981)

The Flavors of the South (1977)

How to Turn a Passion for Food into Profit
(with Elayne Kleeman) (1977)

The Los Angeles Times Natural Foods Cookbook (1973)

The L.A. Gourmet (with Burks Hamner) (1971)

The California Cookbook (1970)

Famous Florida Recipes (1955)